Bible Principles

TURN OLD HABITS INTO NEW HABITS

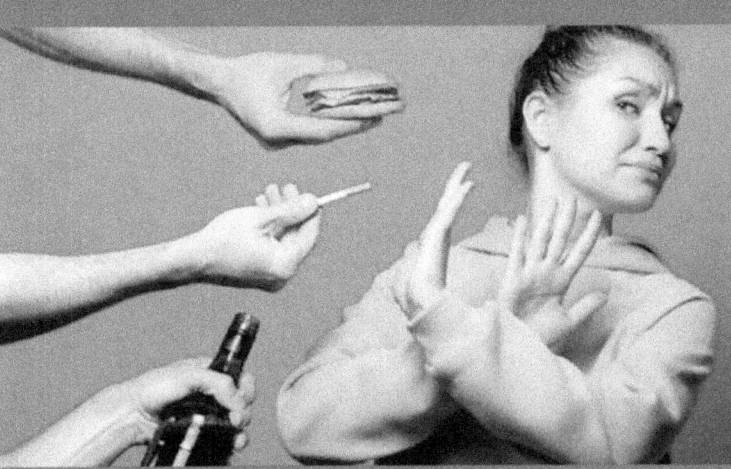

Why and How the Bible Makes a Difference

EDWARD D. ANDREWS

TURN OLD HABITS INTO NEW HABITS

Why and How the Bible Makes a Difference

Edward D. Andrews

Christian Publishing House
Cambridge, Ohio

Copyright © 2023 Edward D. Andrews

All rights reserved. Except for brief quotations in articles, other publications, book reviews, and blogs, no part of this book may be reproduced in any manner without prior written permission from the publishers. For information, write, support@christianpublishers.org

Unless otherwise stated, Scripture quotations are from Updated American Standard Version (UASV) Copyright © 2022 by Christian Publishing House

TURN OLD HABITS INTO NEW HABITS: Why and How the Bible Makes a Difference by Edward D. Andrews

ISBN-10: 1945757736

ISBN-13: 978-1945757730

Table of Contents

Book Description 12
Preface 13
Introduction 15
CHAPTER 1 Why Are Bad Habits So Hard to Break? 17
    Understanding Habits 17
    The Power of Sin 17
    The Role of the Flesh 17
    Neurological Perspective 18
    Breaking Free: The Need for Renewal 18
CHAPTER 2 How Is It Possible to Overcome Bad Habits? 19
    Reliance on God's Strength 19
    Scriptural Meditation and Application 19
    Replacing Bad Habits 19
    Prayer and Fellowship 20
    Hope in Christ 20
    Scriptural Guidance and Inner Reflection 20
    Behavioral Change and the Power of Small Steps 21
    Building a Supportive Environment 21
    Resilience and the Grace of God 21
    Living in the Spirit 22
    Steadfastness in the Word 23
    Establishing Healthy Routines 23
    Supportive Community 24
    Spiritual Armor 24
    Continuous Self-Assessment 24

Reliance on God's Strength 24

Hope in God's Promise 25

CHAPTER 3 How to Get Control Over Your Body and Mind? 26

Committing to God's Sovereignty 26

Daily Prayer and Meditation on the Word 26

Maintaining Physical Health 26

The Role of Cognitive Behavioral Therapy 27

Fostering Spiritual Disciplines 27

Engaging in Purposeful Community 27

Reliance on the Holy Spirit 27

Being Patient and Persistent 28

CHAPTER 4 How Can you Get Control Over Not Getting Enough Sleep? 29

Understanding the Importance of Sleep 29

Strategies for Gaining Control over Sleep 29

CHAPTER 5 How Can You Control Being Overweight? .32

Understanding the Biblical Perspective on the Body 32

Nutrition and Moderation 32

Physical Activity 32

Mindful Eating 33

Supportive Community 33

Addressing Emotional Eating 33

Relying on God's Strength 33

Patience and Consistency 34

CHAPTER 6 How Can You Deal with Destructive Self-Defeating Thoughts? 35

Questions and Answers 35

Recognizing the Power of Thoughts 46

Identifying Negative Thought Patterns 46

Renewing the Mind with the Word of God 46

Replacing Negative Thoughts with God's Truth 46

The Role of Prayer 47

Cultivating Positive Thinking 47

Biblical Counseling and Community Support 47

Relying on the Holy Spirit 48

CHAPTER 7 What Is the Path to Behavioral Change? 49

Questions and Answers 49

Understanding the Need for Change 70

The Role of Repentance 70

Adopting New Behaviors 70

The Power of God's Word 71

Involvement of Community 71

Prayer and Dependence on God 71

Embracing the Process 71

Relying on the Holy Spirit 71

CHAPTER 8 How Do You Get Control Over Anger? 73

Questions and Answer 73

Recognizing and Admitting Anger 84

Understanding the Source of Anger 84

Biblical View of Anger 84

Using God's Word to Counteract Anger 85

Developing New Responses 85

The Role of Forgiveness 85

Prayer and Dependence on God 85

Involvement of Community 85
Relying on the Holy Spirit 86
The Anger Spectrum: Frustration, Annoyance, and Wrath 86
Understanding and Expressing Anger Appropriately 86
Applying the Golden Rule 86
Letting Go of Control 87
Training in Emotional Intelligence 87
The Transforming Power of God's Love 87
Transforming Anger into Positive Action 87
Finding Peace Amidst Anger 88
Recognize Triggers and Symptoms 88
Question Irrational Thoughts 88
Reframe Thoughts 88
Practice Mindfulness 89
Use Relaxation Techniques 89
Assertive Communication 89
Problem-Solving 89
Practicing Forgiveness 90

CHAPTER 9 How Do You Get Control Over Obsessive Control Behaviors? 91

Questions and Answers 91
Christian Counseling, Biblical Counseling, and Biblical Principles 109
Cognitive Behavioral Therapy (CBT) Tools and Practical Tips 111
Build Healthy Relationships 112
Seek Professional Help 112
Christian Counseling and Biblical Principles: Deepening Trust and Surrender 112

Cognitive Behavioral Therapy (CBT) Tools and Practical Tips: Embracing Healthy Control.. 113

CHAPTER 10 How Do You Get Control Over Procrastination? 115

Questions and Answers 115

Christian Counseling and Biblical Principles: Harnessing Proactive Stewardship 116

Cognitive Behavioral Therapy (CBT) Tools and Practical Tips: Cultivating Timely Action 117

CBT Techniques 119

Time Management Techniques 120

CHAPTER 11 How Do You Get Control Over Abuse of Alcohol? 122

Questions and Answers 122

Understanding the Struggle Through a Biblical Lens............ 123

CBT Techniques for Overcoming Alcohol Abuse 124

Restoration through God's Love and Mercy 126

Cognitive-Behavioral Therapy (CBT) Techniques................ 127

CHAPTER 12 How Do You Get Control Overeating? 129

Questions and Answers 129

Biblical and Christian Counseling 130

Cognitive Behavioral Therapy (CBT)............................. 131

CHAPTER 13 How Do You Get Control Over Your Smoking Cigarettes? 133

Questions and Answers 133

Christian Counseling and Biblical Principles 134

Cognitive Behavioral Therapy (CBT) Approach.................. 135

CHAPTER 14 How Do You Get Control Over Your Spending Too Much Time on Social Media? 137

Questions and Answers 137

Christian Counseling and Biblical Principles............................ 138

Cognitive Behavioral Therapy (CBT) Approach..................... 139

CHAPTER 15 How Do You Get Control Over Being Overly Critical or Negative Towards Others?...................................... 141

Questions and Answers 141

Christian Counseling and Biblical Principles............................ 142

Cognitive Behavioral Therapy (CBT) Approach..................... 143

Cognitive Behavioral Therapy (CBT) Approach..................... 145

CHAPTER 16 How Do You Get Control Over Gossiping? 147

Questions and Answers 147

Christian Counseling and Biblical Principles............................ 170

Cognitive Behavioral Therapy (CBT) Approach..................... 171

CHAPTER 17 How Do You Get Control Over Being Consistently Late?... 173

Questions and Answers 173

Biblical Stewardship of Time 174

Cognitive Behavioral Therapy (CBT) Approach..................... 175

CHAPTER 18 How Do You Get Control of Overspending or Not Budgeting Properly? 177

Questions and Answers 177

Biblical Stewardship and Responsibility................................... 178

Cognitive Behavioral Therapy (CBT) Approach..................... 179

CHAPTER 19 How Do You Get Control Over Being a Chronic Complainer? 181

Questions and Answers 181

Biblical Perspective on Complaining... 182

Cognitive Behavioral Therapy (CBT) Perspective and Tools 183

CHAPTER 20 How Do You Get Control Over Not Listening Actively to Others? 185

    Questions and Answers 185

    The Biblical Imperative of Active Listening 186

    Cognitive Behavioral Therapy (CBT) Approach to Active Listening 187

CHAPTER 21 How Do You Get Control Over Holding Grudges? 189

    Questions and Answers 189

    The Biblical Perspective on Holding Grudges 190

    Cognitive Behavioral Therapy (CBT) Approach to Releasing Grudges 191

CHAPTER 22 How Do You Get Control Over Your Pornography Addiction? 193

    Questions and Answers 193

    Overcoming Pornography Addiction Through Biblical Principles and Counsel 206

    Cognitive Behavioral Therapy (CBT) Approach to Overcoming Pornography Addiction 207

CHAPTER 23 How Do You Get Control Over Your Masturbation Habit? 209

    Questions and Answers 209

    Overcoming a Habit of Masturbation Through Biblical Principles and Counsel 215

    Cognitive Behavioral Therapy (CBT) Approach to Overcoming a Masturbation Habit 216

Edward D. Andrews

Book Description

In "TURN OLD HABITS INTO NEW HABITS: Why and How the Bible Makes a Difference," the power of scriptural truth and professional psychological insights meld to create a transformative guide for those seeking change. This book is for those wrestling with habitual behaviors that hamper their spiritual growth and personal development. It offers hope and actionable advice, providing readers with the tools to understand and overcome habits that might seem insurmountable.

Drawing from a wide range of behavioral issues, from procrastination to obsessive control behaviors, alcohol abuse to negativity towards others, this comprehensive guide shines a biblical light on common struggles. It provides a Christian perspective on each issue, with pertinent scripture and exploration of the original Greek and Hebrew meanings, encouraging readers to renovate their minds with God's word.

Coupled with Christian counseling and biblical principles, this book presents Cognitive Behavioral Therapy (CBT) tools and practical tips, a scientifically backed method to understand and modify harmful behaviors. Each chapter breaks down a specific issue, presenting insightful questions and answers and providing deep biblical understanding and actionable CBT techniques.

"TURN OLD HABITS INTO NEW HABITS" is more than a book; it is a path to transformation. It allows readers to reflect, understand, and eventually gain control over their destructive patterns. In these pages, readers will find an unwavering belief in their potential to change, underpinned by God's strength and the therapeutic power of psychology. Whatever the habit, change is possible, and this book serves as a vital companion on that journey.

Preface

In the quiet of our hearts, we often wrestle with habits that obstruct our paths to fulfillment and peace, habits that, regardless of our best efforts, cling to us stubbornly. It is for those enduring this struggle that "TURN OLD HABITS INTO NEW HABITS: Why and How the Bible Makes a Difference" was written. This book aims not only to shed light on these shadows but also to provide the tools for lasting transformation.

The inspiration behind this book is born from an understanding that our internal battles are not solely personal or isolated; they are shared by countless others. While the nature of our habits may vary, our shared humanity connects us all. We all strive for change and growth, yearning to escape the clutches of the habits that impede our personal and spiritual development.

This book attempts to bridge the wisdom of scripture and the insights of cognitive behavioral therapy, creating a rich tapestry of spiritual and psychological understanding. By turning to the Bible, we unearth divine wisdom, which can illuminate our journey towards self-improvement. Simultaneously, cognitive behavioral therapy provides a pragmatic and scientifically supported approach to understanding and modifying our behavioral patterns.

As you journey through this book, remember, change is a process. It is a winding road rather than a straight path. This book is not a quick fix; it is an invitation to start a transformative journey that requires commitment, patience, and resilience. It is a call to engage with the depth of scripture and the insights of cognitive behavioral therapy with openness and courage.

In the pages that follow, you will find not just theories and ideas but also practical advice, questions for reflection, and tools for change. I pray that this book will be a resource for you, providing support, understanding, and encouragement as you strive to break old habits and nurture new ones. Above all, I hope this book will bring you closer to the person you aspire to be in God's sight.

Here is to a journey of transformation, grace, and renewal.

Edward D. Andrews

Chief Translator of the Updated American Standard Version

Introduction

Welcome to the beginning of a transformative journey. This book, "TURN OLD HABITS INTO NEW HABITS: Why and How the Bible Makes a Difference", seeks to help you engage more meaningfully in your process of personal growth. It is an opportunity to connect with God, yourself, and the patterns of behavior that shape your daily life.

As you turn these pages, you will embark on an exploration of the intricate relationship between spiritual truth and psychological understanding. The chapters are designed to guide you through various challenges, using the wisdom of the Bible and the principles of cognitive behavioral therapy. You will engage with time-honored biblical teachings and modern therapeutic approaches, and learn how these two seemingly different areas can intersect to facilitate profound personal change.

The unique value of this book is in its integrative approach. It demonstrates how Scripture provides an enduring moral and spiritual compass, while cognitive behavioral therapy offers us tools to understand and manage our thoughts, feelings, and behaviors. This blend of the spiritual and the scientific is what makes this book a unique resource in the journey to break old habits and cultivate new ones.

Each chapter focuses on a specific issue, beginning with an overview of the problem, followed by an in-depth exploration of biblical principles related to the issue at hand. You'll then delve into cognitive behavioral strategies tailored to the specific habit or pattern you're working to change. This structure is designed to offer you a comprehensive understanding of the issue and equip you with practical tools for change.

While the content of this book is structured and detailed, the journey of change is deeply personal and unique to each individual. Therefore, it is essential to approach this book as a starting point, a guide that can help orient you and offer support as you navigate your path of transformation. As you read, consider how the biblical principles and cognitive behavioral therapy techniques resonate with you. Reflect on what feels relevant, challenging, or inspiring, and explore how these insights might translate into your daily life.

Remember, the journey to replace old habits with new ones isn't a sprint; it's a marathon. It involves patience, persistence, and grace towards oneself. As you journey through the pages of this book, be gentle with yourself, recognizing that growth takes time, and setbacks are a natural part of the process. Lean into God's unending grace and mercy, trusting that His love is constant amidst your struggles and triumphs.

May this book be a beacon guiding you towards a renewed sense of self, one marked by growth, resilience, and a closer relationship with God. May it offer you hope and practical tools in your ongoing quest for transformation, and may it be a reminder that you are never alone in your struggles. As you turn these pages, remember that God is with you, cheering you on every step of the way.

CHAPTER 1 Why Are Bad Habits So Hard to Break?

Understanding Habits

Habits, both good and bad, are deeply ingrained in our routines, largely because they stem from the brain's tendency to optimize its tasks. According to Cognitive Behavioral Therapy (CBT), our brain's neural pathways become strengthened with repetition, making habitual behavior second nature.

In the context of the Scriptures, even Paul the Apostle acknowledged this struggle against habitual sins. In Romans 7:15 (ESV), he confessed, "For I do not understand my own actions. For I do not do what I want, but I do the very thing I hate."

The Power of Sin

Sin is a fundamental concept in understanding why bad habits are difficult to break. The Bible describes sin as a powerful force that can enslave us (Romans 6:16, ESV). Bad habits often have roots in sin, which can take hold and dictate our actions, sometimes subconsciously.

The Role of the Flesh

The Bible further explains this struggle with bad habits through the concept of the "flesh." Galatians 5:17 (ESV) says, "For the desires of the flesh are against the Spirit, and the desires of the Spirit are against the flesh, for these are opposed to each other, to keep you from doing the things you want to do." Our fleshly desires often contribute to the formation of bad habits.

Neurological Perspective

From a cognitive behavioral perspective, when we repeat a bad habit, the neurons in our brain create a strong, interconnected network. This forms a kind of 'shortcut' for our brain, making it easier to continue the habit than to break it. Therefore, when we try to stop, we are essentially working against our own brain's wiring.

Breaking Free: The Need for Renewal

Breaking bad habits isn't easy, but it is not impossible. The key lies in the renewal of our minds and our reliance on God's strength. According to Romans 12:2 (ESV), "Do not be conformed to this world, but be transformed by the renewal of your mind, that by testing you may discern what is the will of God, what is good and acceptable and perfect." In this way, we begin to understand how the Bible can make a profound difference in transforming old habits into new ones.

CHAPTER 2 How Is It Possible to Overcome Bad Habits?

Reliance on God's Strength

Overcoming bad habits begins with acknowledging our own limitations and turning to God for help. The apostle Paul makes it clear in 2 Corinthians 12:9 (ESV), "But he said to me, 'My grace is sufficient for you, for my power is made perfect in weakness.' Therefore I will boast all the more gladly of my weaknesses, so that the power of Christ may rest upon me." We can rely on God's strength when our human efforts fall short.

Scriptural Meditation and Application

By meditating on Scripture and applying it to our lives, we can use God's Word as a powerful tool to combat bad habits. Psalm 119:11 (ASV) encourages us, "Thy word have I laid up in my heart, that I might not sin against thee." By internalizing Scripture, we set up a defense against sin and temptation.

Replacing Bad Habits

Rather than simply trying to "stop" a bad habit, cognitive behavioral therapy suggests replacing it with a healthier behavior. Similarly, in Ephesians 4:22-24 (ESV), Paul instructs us, "to put off your old self, which belongs to your former manner of life and is corrupt through deceitful desires, and to be renewed in the spirit of your minds, and to put on the new self, created after the likeness of God in true righteousness and holiness." This implies not just discarding our old, sinful behaviors but also embracing new, godly habits.

Prayer and Fellowship

Prayer and fellowship with other believers play essential roles in overcoming bad habits. James 5:16 (ESV) encourages, "Therefore, confess your sins to one another and pray for one another, that you may be healed. The prayer of a righteous person has great power as it is working." By leaning into our community and God through prayer, we can find support and accountability in our journey of transformation.

Hope in Christ

Ultimately, our hope in overcoming bad habits lies in our relationship with Jesus Christ. As we grow closer to Him, we become more like Him, shedding our old habits in favor of new, Christlike ones. As Paul affirms in Philippians 4:13 (ESV), "I can do all things through him who strengthens me," we too can find the strength to overcome our bad habits through Christ.

Scriptural Guidance and Inner Reflection

Biblical Counseling and Cognitive Behavioral Therapy both encourage self-reflection. This involves reviewing our thoughts and behaviors, identifying areas of weakness, and understanding how they align with our values and beliefs. With Scripture as our guide, we can draw upon the wisdom of Proverbs 4:23 (ESV), which instructs us to "Keep your heart with all vigilance, for from it flow the springs of life."

Engaging in regular self-reflection helps us understand our triggers and motivations, allowing us to anticipate and manage situations that tempt us towards our bad habits. This reflection can be done through journaling, prayer, and meditation on Scripture.

Behavioral Change and the Power of Small Steps

Overcoming bad habits is often a gradual process rather than an immediate change. Cognitive Behavioral Therapy emphasizes the importance of taking small steps towards your goal. In line with this, we can consider Zechariah 4:10 (ASV), which reminds us, "For who hath despised the day of small things?" Even small changes are valuable and can lead to significant transformation over time.

When we feel overwhelmed by the thought of completely eliminating a bad habit, we can start by making small changes. For example, reducing the frequency of the habit, introducing a healthier behavior as a replacement, or changing the environment associated with the habit. Over time, these changes can add up to a complete transformation.

Building a Supportive Environment

Creating an environment that supports our goal of overcoming bad habits is essential. This includes physical spaces, relationships, and spiritual communities. Hebrews 10:24-25 (ESV) encourages us to "consider how to stir up one another to love and good works, not neglecting to meet together, as is the habit of some, but encouraging one another..."

Building a supportive community provides accountability, encouragement, and companionship during our journey. Regularly attending church, joining Bible study groups, and seeking Christian counseling can contribute to this supportive environment.

Resilience and the Grace of God

Despite our best efforts, there will be times when we stumble. However, the grace of God is always available to us. As declared in Lamentations 3:22-23 (ASV), "It is of Jehovah's lovingkindnesses that we are not consumed, because his compassions fail not. They are new every morning; great is thy faithfulness." We can find solace in God's unwavering faithfulness and mercy.

During these moments, resilience is crucial. Instead of focusing on the setback, we can see it as an opportunity to learn and adapt our strategies. Each failure brings us closer to understanding what works best for us.

Living in the Spirit

Galatians 5:22-23 (ESV) reminds us of the fruits of living in the Spirit, "But the fruit of the Spirit is love, joy, peace, patience, kindness, goodness, faithfulness, gentleness, self-control; against such things there is no law." By fostering these fruits in our lives, we naturally begin to replace our bad habits with behaviors that align with the Spirit's work in us.

Each of these approaches forms a comprehensive strategy for overcoming bad habits. While it may be challenging, remember that transformation is a journey. With faith and perseverance, change is not only possible, but promised, through the strength and grace of God.

CHAPTER 3 What Is Needed to Prevent the Return of Bad Habits?

Steadfastness in the Word

An essential element in preventing the return of bad habits is remaining steadfast in God's Word. Joshua 1:8 (ASV) instructs, "This book of the law shall not depart out of thy mouth, but thou shalt meditate thereon day and night, that thou mayest observe to do according to all that is written therein." Regularly studying, meditating, and applying Scripture in our daily lives is a powerful tool in maintaining new habits.

This steadfastness extends to prayer. Maintain an open line of communication with God, being honest about your struggles. God, who knows our hearts and minds, provides guidance and strength in our fight against recurring bad habits.

Establishing Healthy Routines

Establishing and maintaining healthy routines is crucial in preventing old habits from returning. Consider Daniel, who despite significant pressure, stayed true to his prayer routine, as described in Daniel 6:10 (ASV). Following a consistent routine can provide structure and discourage the revival of unhealthy habits.

Use tools from Cognitive Behavioral Therapy to establish these routines. Start with clear, achievable goals, and gradually expand them as you grow more comfortable and confident. Ensure these routines include aspects of physical health, such as regular exercise, a balanced diet, and sufficient sleep, as these can directly impact your ability to resist falling back into old habits.

Supportive Community

Having a supportive community is invaluable. Hebrews 10:24-25 (ESV) emphasizes the importance of not neglecting to meet together and encouraging one another. Surrounding yourself with positive influences who can offer encouragement, prayer, and guidance can help safeguard against the resurgence of negative habits. Regular fellowship allows for accountability and provides a safe space to share and overcome struggles together.

Spiritual Armor

Ephesians 6:10-18 (ESV) describes the spiritual armor of God. It includes truth, righteousness, the gospel of peace, faith, salvation, and the Word of God as our defense mechanisms. Equipping ourselves with this spiritual armor is vital in preventing old, negative habits from taking hold again. This armor equips us with strength and defense against potential setbacks.

Continuous Self-Assessment

Frequent self-assessment allows you to remain aware of your thoughts, emotions, and actions. In Lamentations 3:40 (ASV), we are encouraged to "Let us search and try our ways, and turn again to the Lord." This ongoing self-evaluation ensures that we remain vigilant and proactive in maintaining our new habits and preventing the return of the old ones.

Reliance on God's Strength

Always remember to lean on God's strength. The Apostle Paul reminds us in Philippians 4:13 (ESV), "I can do all things through him who strengthens me." Even as we work to prevent the return of bad habits, we must remember that our strength comes from the Lord. We are not facing these challenges alone, and with God's strength, we have the power to resist and overcome.

Hope in God's Promise

Finally, never lose sight of God's promises. We have a hope that transcends our current circumstances. 2 Corinthians 5:17 (ESV) promises, "Therefore, if anyone is in Christ, he is a new creation. The old has passed away; behold, the new has come." God is continually at work in us, refining us, and helping us to grow into the likeness of Christ.

Preventing the return of bad habits is an ongoing commitment. It requires diligence, self-awareness, reliance on God, and the support of a faith-filled community. However, the effort is worth it, as the transformation brings us closer to living a life fully in line with God's Word and His intentions for us.

CHAPTER 3 How to Get Control Over Your Body and Mind?

Committing to God's Sovereignty

As Christians, we believe in God's sovereignty over every aspect of our lives, including our bodies and minds. Romans 12:1-2 (ESV) urges, "I appeal to you therefore, brothers, by the mercies of God, to present your bodies as a living sacrifice, holy and acceptable to God, which is your spiritual worship. Do not be conformed to this world, but be transformed by the renewal of your mind."

Daily Prayer and Meditation on the Word

Communicating with God through prayer and meditating on His Word is a powerful way to control our body and mind. As we immerse ourselves in God's Word, we open ourselves to His guidance and wisdom. Psalm 119:105 (ASV) affirms, "Thy word is a lamp unto my feet, and a light unto my path."

Maintaining Physical Health

Caring for our physical health is a vital part of controlling our body. This means maintaining a balanced diet, exercising regularly, ensuring we get enough sleep, and avoiding harmful substances. 1 Corinthians 6:19-20 (ESV) reminds us, "Or do you not know that your body is a temple of the Holy Spirit within you, whom you have from God? You are not your own, for you were bought with a price. So glorify God in your body."

The Role of Cognitive Behavioral Therapy

Cognitive Behavioral Therapy (CBT) provides practical strategies to help control our thoughts and actions. CBT encourages us to identify harmful thought patterns and replace them with healthier ones. Philippians 4:8 (ESV) gives a biblical counterpart to this idea: "Finally, brothers, whatever is true, whatever is honorable, whatever is just, whatever is pure, whatever is lovely, whatever is commendable, if there is any excellence, if there is anything worthy of praise, think about these things."

Fostering Spiritual Disciplines

Cultivating spiritual disciplines, like fasting, solitude, and silence, can help in exercising control over our bodies and minds. These practices help us shift our focus from our physical desires and needs to our spiritual growth and relationship with God. Matthew 6:17-18 (ASV) provides guidance on how to approach these disciplines, "But thou, when thou fastest, anoint thy head, and wash thy face; that thou be not seen of men to fast, but of thy Father who is in secret: and thy Father, who seeth in secret, shall recompense thee."

Engaging in Purposeful Community

Joining a supportive and faith-filled community offers accountability, encouragement, and guidance. It allows us to learn from each other's experiences and grow together in faith. Hebrews 10:24-25 (ESV) underscores this, "And let us consider how to stir up one another to love and good works, not neglecting to meet together, as is the habit of some, but encouraging one another."

Reliance on the Holy Spirit

While we strive to control our bodies and minds, we must remember the role of the Holy Spirit in this endeavor. Galatians 5:22-

23 (ESV) shares, "But the fruit of the Spirit is love, joy, peace, patience, kindness, goodness, faithfulness, gentleness, self-control; against such things there is no law." As we yield to the Spirit, we find that He produces these fruits within us, helping us to gain mastery over our bodies and minds.

Being Patient and Persistent

Finally, it's important to be patient with yourself. Changing thought patterns and behaviors takes time. 2 Peter 3:9 (ASV) encourages us, "The Lord is not slack concerning his promise, as some count slackness; but is longsuffering to you-ward, not wishing that any should perish, but that all should come to repentance." Just as God is patient with us, we should also be patient with ourselves, trusting in God's timing and His transformative work in us.

In conclusion, gaining control over your body and mind involves an integrated approach of spiritual discipline, physical care, community support, cognitive strategies, and above all, reliance on God's Word and the work of the Holy Spirit. It's a journey of perseverance, faith, and continuous growth.

CHAPTER 4 How Can you Get Control Over Not Getting Enough Sleep?

Sleep is a critical component of overall health and well-being. In fact, inadequate sleep can lead to a myriad of health complications ranging from diminished cognitive function to chronic conditions such as diabetes and heart disease (CDC, 2020). Despite these realities, many individuals struggle to attain the recommended amount of nightly sleep. This article seeks to provide evidence-based strategies to help you gain control over not getting enough sleep.

Understanding the Importance of Sleep

Before delving into the strategies, it's essential to comprehend the importance of sleep. The National Sleep Foundation (2020) recommends that adults get between seven to nine hours of sleep each night. During sleep, the body performs crucial restorative functions such as consolidating memory, regulating hormones, repairing tissues, and maintaining the immune system. Consequently, consistently receiving insufficient sleep could lead to cognitive impairments, emotional issues, and increased susceptibility to infections (Walker, 2017).

Strategies for Gaining Control over Sleep

1. **Establish a Regular Sleep Schedule**: Irregular sleep patterns can disrupt your body's internal clock, or circadian rhythm, leading to sleep issues. One of the most effective ways to improve sleep is to maintain a regular sleep schedule, going to

bed and waking up at the same time every day, even on weekends (American Sleep Association, 2020).

2. **Create a Sleep-friendly Environment**: Your bedroom environment can significantly impact your sleep quality. The room should be dark, quiet, and cool. Consider using earplugs, eye shades, or white noise machines if necessary. Moreover, invest in a comfortable mattress and pillows (National Sleep Foundation, 2020).

3. **Limit Exposure to Light Before Bed**: Exposure to bright lights, particularly blue light from electronic devices, can interfere with your body's production of melatonin, a hormone that regulates sleep (Harvard Medical School, 2019). Avoid using electronic devices like computers, smartphones, or televisions for at least an hour before bedtime.

4. **Exercise Regularly**: Regular physical activity can help you fall asleep faster and enjoy deeper sleep. However, avoid vigorous exercise close to bedtime as it might interfere with your sleep (Johns Hopkins Medicine, n.d.).

5. **Manage Stress**: High stress levels can impede your sleep. Techniques like mindfulness, meditation, deep breathing, yoga, or progressive muscle relaxation can help you manage stress and promote better sleep (Mayo Clinic, 2020).

6. **Monitor Your Diet**: What you eat and drink can affect your sleep. Avoid large meals, caffeine, and alcohol close to bedtime. While alcohol might make you feel sleepy initially, it can disrupt your sleep later in the night (National Sleep Foundation, 2020).

7. **Consider Cognitive Behavioral Therapy for Insomnia (CBT-I)**: If you're still struggling with sleep issues, consider CBT-I. This structured program helps you identify and replace thoughts and behaviors that cause or worsen sleep problems with habits that promote sound sleep (American Academy of Sleep Medicine, 2018).

Conclusion

In summary, getting sufficient sleep is a crucial aspect of maintaining optimal health and well-being. While it might seem challenging to gain control over your sleep, implementing the above strategies can significantly enhance your sleep quality and quantity. However, if you continue to struggle with sleep issues despite implementing these strategies, it is recommended that you consult with a healthcare provider or a sleep specialist to rule out any underlying sleep disorders.

CHAPTER 5 How Can You Control Being Overweight?

Understanding the Biblical Perspective on the Body

The Bible views our bodies as temples of the Holy Spirit. As 1 Corinthians 6:19-20 (ESV) states, "Or do you not know that your body is a temple of the Holy Spirit within you, whom you have from God? You are not your own, for you were bought with a price. So glorify God in your body." This verse underscores the importance of treating our bodies with respect and care, which includes maintaining a healthy weight.

Nutrition and Moderation

Proverbs 25:27 (ASV) warns, "It is not good to eat much honey: So for men to search out their own glory is grievous." While this verse is not directly about physical health, it presents a principle of balance and moderation that applies to our eating habits. Consuming a balanced diet full of fruits, vegetables, lean proteins, and whole grains can significantly help control weight. Remember, it's not about banning certain foods but enjoying them in moderation.

Physical Activity

Regular physical activity is a crucial part of maintaining a healthy weight. Exercise not only helps burn calories but also boosts your mood and overall well-being. In 1 Timothy 4:8 (ESV), we read, "For while bodily training is of some value, godliness is of value in every way, as it holds promise for the present life and also for the life to come." While this verse primarily highlights the importance of spiritual training, it also acknowledges the value of physical training.

Mindful Eating

The principles of Cognitive Behavioral Therapy (CBT) suggest mindful eating as a tool to control weight. Mindful eating involves paying full attention to the experience of eating and drinking, both inside and outside the body. It is about noticing the colors, smells, flavors, and textures of your food; chewing slowly; getting rid of distractions; and learning to cope with guilt and anxiety about food. Ecclesiastes 9:7 (ASV) invites, "Go thy way, eat thy bread with joy, and drink thy wine with a merry heart; for God hath already accepted thy works." This verse can be viewed as a call to conscious, joyful consumption.

Supportive Community

A supportive community plays a vital role in managing weight. Involving others in your journey can offer much-needed encouragement and accountability. As described in Ecclesiastes 4:9-10 (ESV), "Two are better than one, because they have a good reward for their toil. For if they fall, one will lift up his fellow."

Addressing Emotional Eating

Biblical counseling can help individuals address emotional eating. Often, people turn to food for comfort when they feel stressed, anxious, or upset. However, Psalm 34:18 (ESV) reassures, "The Lord is near to the brokenhearted and saves the crushed in spirit." Understanding that God's comfort surpasses any temporary relief food provides can be a powerful step in controlling weight.

Relying on God's Strength

Controlling weight often involves breaking old habits and establishing new ones. This process can be challenging, but we are not alone in our struggle. Philippians 4:13 (ESV) encourages, "I can do all things through him who strengthens me." Relying on God's strength is fundamental in successfully controlling weight.

Patience and Consistency

Weight control is not a quick fix but a journey requiring patience and consistency. In James 1:4 (ASV), we are encouraged, "And let patience have its perfect work, that ye may be perfect and entire, lacking in nothing." Similarly, it's essential to approach weight management with patience, understanding that real change takes time.

In conclusion, controlling weight from a Biblical perspective involves an integrative approach—healthy eating habits, regular physical activity, emotional resilience, community support, mindful eating, and a deep reliance on God's strength. It's a journey of self-care that helps you honor God with your body.

See my book: HOW TO MANAGE YOUR FITNESS 101: Making Your Body Work for You. ISBN: 979-8387182983

(https://www.amazon.com/dp/B0BYM1257B)

CHAPTER 6 How Can You Deal with Destructive Self-Defeating Thoughts?

Questions and Answers

What is "the old person"? (Romans 6:6; Ephesians 4:22-24; Colossians 3:9-10)

Understanding "the Old Person"

In several biblical passages, such as Romans 6:6, Ephesians 4:22-24, and Colossians 3:9-10, the term "the old person" refers to the former self or the sinful nature that believers have put off through their union with Christ. It represents the unregenerate state characterized by disobedience and rebellion against God. Let's explore these verses to gain a deeper understanding.

Romans 6:6

Romans 6:6 (ASV) states, "Knowing this, that our old man was crucified with him, that the body of sin might be done away, that so we should no longer be in bondage to sin."

In this passage, "the old man" represents the sinful nature inherited from Adam. Through the death and resurrection of Jesus Christ, believers are united with Him, and their old self is considered crucified. This signifies that the power of sin over their lives has been broken, enabling them to live a new life in Christ.

Ephesians 4:22-24

Ephesians 4:22-24 (ESV) says, "to put off your old self, which belongs to your former manner of life and is corrupt through deceitful desires, and to be renewed in the spirit of your minds, and to put on the new self, created after the likeness of God in true righteousness and holiness."

Here, "the old self" refers to the previous way of living before coming to faith in Christ. It represents the corrupt and sinful nature governed by deceitful desires. Believers are called to put off this old self and be renewed in their minds by the Holy Spirit. They are to embrace the new self, which reflects the righteousness and holiness that comes from God.

Colossians 3:9-10

Colossians 3:9-10 (ASV) states, "lie not one to another; seeing that ye have put off the old man with his doings, and have put on the new man, that is being renewed unto knowledge after the image of him that created him."

In this passage, "the old man" represents the former self associated with sinful behavior. Believers are instructed not to lie to one another since they have already put off the old self along with its sinful actions. Instead, they are to put on the new self, which is continually being renewed in knowledge according to the image of God who created them.

Key Insights

- The old person or old self refers to the unregenerate state characterized by sin and rebellion against God.
- Through their union with Christ, believers have put off the old self and its sinful nature.
- The old self is crucified, enabling believers to no longer be in bondage to sin.
- Believers are called to put off the old self, be renewed in their minds, and put on the new self, which reflects righteousness and holiness.
- The new self is continually being renewed in knowledge and conformed to the image of God.

Understanding the concept of "the old person" helps believers grasp the transformation they have undergone through their faith in Christ and the ongoing process of sanctification as they strive to live in accordance with their new identity in Him.

Why should we "take off the old person"?

The Bible teaches the importance of "taking off the old person" or putting away our former self characterized by sinful behaviors. This transformative process is essential for believers as they seek to align their lives with God's standards and live in accordance with their new identity in Christ.

Scriptural Support:

- Ephesians 4:22-24 (ESV): "to put off your old self, which belongs to your former manner of life and is corrupt through deceitful desires, and to be renewed in the spirit of your minds, and to put on the new self, created after the likeness of God in true righteousness and holiness."

Recognizing the Former Manner of Life

By "taking off the old person," we acknowledge and reject the former manner of life characterized by sinful behaviors. This includes attitudes, thoughts, and actions contrary to God's standards. It involves recognizing the corrupt nature of the old self, influenced by deceitful desires that lead away from God's truth.

Seeking Renewal in the Mind

In putting off the old self, we are called to be renewed in the spirit of our minds. This renewal involves a transformation in our thought patterns, attitudes, and worldview. It is a process guided by the Holy Spirit, aligning our minds with God's truth, and reshaping our thinking according to His Word. Through this renewal, we gain a deeper understanding of God's righteousness and holiness.

Putting on the New Self

Taking off the old person is not merely a removal of negative behaviors; it also involves putting on the new self. The new self reflects the image of God and is created in true righteousness and holiness. It embodies the transformed nature of believers who have been reconciled to God through faith in Christ. Putting on the new self entails embracing godly attitudes, thoughts, and behaviors that align with our new identity in Christ.

Motivation for Transformation

There are several reasons why we should "take off the old person":

1. Obedience to God: We are called to live in obedience to God's commands, and shedding the old self is an act of obedience and surrender to His will.

2. Reflecting God's Image: As bearers of God's image, we are called to reflect His righteousness and holiness. By taking off the old self, we align ourselves with His character and bring glory to His name.

3. Spiritual Growth: Removing the old person is essential for our spiritual growth and maturity. It enables us to grow in Christlikeness and experience the fullness of life in Him.

4. Witness to Others: Our transformed lives serve as a powerful testimony to the world. By putting off the old self and embracing the new self, we become living examples of God's redemptive work and His transformative power.

In summary, "taking off the old person" involves recognizing and rejecting our former manner of life, seeking renewal in the mind, and embracing the new self created in righteousness and holiness. This process is vital for believers as they strive to live in accordance with God's standards, grow spiritually, and serve as witnesses of His transformative power.

How can we "take off" the old person and keep it off?

How Can We "Take Off" the Old Person and Keep It Off?

The Bible teaches us not only to "take off" the old person, but also to keep it off, ensuring a consistent transformation in our lives. This process involves ongoing renewal, relying on the power of the Holy Spirit, and actively cultivating godly attitudes and behaviors. Let's explore some key principles and Scriptures that guide us in this journey.

Scriptural Support:

- Ephesians 4:22-24 (ESV): "to put off your old self, which belongs to your former manner of life and is corrupt through deceitful desires, and to be renewed in the spirit of your minds, and to put on the new self, created after the likeness of God in true righteousness and holiness."

Constant Renewal

Taking off the old person and keeping it off requires constant renewal. We are called to be renewed in the spirit of our minds, allowing the Holy Spirit to continually transform our thoughts, attitudes, and perspectives. This renewal comes through the consistent study and meditation on God's Word, prayer, and fellowship with other believers. It involves surrendering our minds to the guidance and influence of the Holy Spirit.

Walking in the Spirit

To keep the old person off, we need to walk in the Spirit and rely on His empowering presence. Galatians 5:16 (ESV) states, "But I say, walk by the Spirit, and you will not gratify the desires of the flesh." By submitting to the leading of the Holy Spirit, we gain the strength and guidance to resist the temptations and influences of the old nature. This involves maintaining a close relationship with God, seeking His guidance and wisdom in every aspect of our lives.

Putting on the New Self

Keeping the old person off requires actively putting on the new self. As mentioned in Ephesians 4:24, the new self is created after the likeness of God in true righteousness and holiness. This involves cultivating godly attitudes, virtues, and behaviors that reflect our new identity in Christ. We strive to imitate Christ, embracing His love, forgiveness, humility, and compassion in our interactions with others. This transformation is not a one-time event but a continual process of growth and maturity in our walk with God.

Accountability and Community

Maintaining accountability and being part of a supportive community are crucial in keeping the old person off. Hebrews 10:24-25 (ESV) encourages us to "consider how to stir up one another to love and good works, not neglecting to meet together, as is the habit of some, but encouraging one another." By surrounding ourselves with fellow believers who share our commitment to living according to God's standards, we can support and challenge one another in our spiritual journey.

Personal Discipline and Surrender

Personal discipline and surrender are essential in keeping the old person off. We must discipline ourselves to guard our minds and hearts, to resist sinful influences, and to pursue righteousness. This involves making intentional choices aligned with God's Word and relying on His grace to empower us. It also requires a daily surrender of our will and desires to God, allowing Him to work in and through us for His glory.

What is "the new person"? (Romans 6:6; Ephesians 4:22-24; Colossians 3:9-10)

The concept of "the new person" refers to the transformed identity and nature of believers in Christ. It represents the spiritual renewal and change that occurs when someone accepts Jesus as their Savior and follows Him. The new person is characterized by righteousness, holiness, and conformity to the image of Christ.

Scriptural Support:

- Romans 6:6 (ESV): "We know that our old self was crucified with him in order that the body of sin might be brought to nothing, so that we would no longer be enslaved to sin."
- Ephesians 4:22-24 (ESV): "to put off your old self, which belongs to your former manner of life and is corrupt through deceitful desires, and to be renewed in the spirit of your minds, and to put on the new self, created after the likeness of God in true righteousness and holiness."
- Colossians 3:9-10 (ESV): "Do not lie to one another, seeing that you have put off the old self with its practices and have put on the new self, which is being renewed in knowledge after the image of its creator."

Crucifixion of the Old Self

The new person emerges through the crucifixion of the old self. Romans 6:6 emphasizes that our old self was crucified with Christ. This signifies the breaking of the power of sin and the release from its bondage. The old self, characterized by sinful desires and practices, is put to death so that we may no longer be enslaved to sin. It is through the work of Christ on the cross that our old self is crucified and rendered powerless.

Renewal in the Spirit of the Mind

As we put off the old self, we are called to be renewed in the spirit of our minds. Ephesians 4:22-24 highlights the ongoing process of renewal, where our minds are transformed and aligned with the mind of Christ. This renewal comes through the work of the Holy Spirit, who enables us to think and act in accordance with God's truth. The new self is created after the likeness of God, reflecting true righteousness and holiness.

Putting on the New Self

Putting on the new self involves embracing our transformed identity in Christ. Colossians 3:9-10 instructs us not to lie to one another because we have put off the old self with its practices and put on the new self. This new self is continually renewed in knowledge, conforming to the image of its Creator. It reflects the character and nature of God, displaying righteousness, truth, love, and holiness in our words and actions.

Conforming to the Image of Christ

The new person is being conformed to the image of Christ. This means that our character, attitudes, and behaviors are transformed to resemble those of Jesus. The process of becoming like Christ involves daily growth and conformity through the power of the Holy Spirit and the influence of God's Word. It is a lifelong journey of becoming more Christlike in our thoughts, words, and actions.

In summary, the new person represents the transformed identity and nature of believers in Christ. It involves the crucifixion of the old self, renewal in the spirit of the mind, putting on the new self, and conforming to the image of Christ. Through the work of the Holy Spirit, believers are continually renewed and transformed to reflect the righteousness, holiness, and character of God in their lives.

How can we put on the new person?

Putting on the new person involves actively embracing and living out our transformed identity in Christ. It requires intentional steps and choices that align with our new nature in Him. The Scriptures provide guidance on how we can put on the new person and walk in the righteousness and holiness that comes from God.

Scriptural Support:

- Ephesians 4:22-24 (ESV): "to put off your old self, which belongs to your former manner of life and is corrupt through deceitful desires, and to be renewed in the spirit of your minds, and to put on the new self, created after the likeness of God in true righteousness and holiness."

- Colossians 3:12-14 (ESV): "Put on then, as God's chosen ones, holy and beloved, compassionate hearts, kindness, humility, meekness, and patience, bearing with one another and, if one has a complaint against another, forgiving each other; as the Lord has forgiven you, so you also must forgive. And above all these put on love, which binds everything together in perfect harmony."

Put Off the Old Self

To put on the new person, we first need to put off the old self. Ephesians 4:22-24 instructs us to consciously let go of our former manner of life that was corrupted by deceitful desires. This involves turning away from sinful behaviors, attitudes, and habits that are inconsistent with our new identity in Christ. Through the power of the Holy Spirit, we can shed our old self and embrace the transformation that comes from being united with Christ.

Be Renewed in the Spirit of Your Minds

Renewal is a crucial aspect of putting on the new person. Ephesians 4:23 urges us to be renewed in the spirit of our minds. This renewal takes place through the ongoing work of the Holy Spirit, who transforms our thinking, attitudes, and perspectives to align with God's truth. It involves feeding our minds with God's Word, meditating on His promises, and seeking His guidance and wisdom. As we allow the Holy Spirit to renew our minds, our thoughts and actions will increasingly reflect the righteousness and holiness of our new nature in Christ.

Put On the New Self

Putting on the new person also requires actively embracing the virtues and characteristics that reflect our transformed identity. Colossians 3:12-14 provides a list of qualities that we are to put on: compassion, kindness, humility, meekness, patience, forgiveness, and above all, love. These virtues should mark our interactions with others and our daily conduct. By intentionally cultivating these qualities in our lives, we demonstrate the new person and allow the love and righteousness of Christ to flow through us.

Continual Transformation

Putting on the new person is not a one-time event but a continual process. It involves daily choices, reliance on the Holy Spirit, and a commitment to live in accordance with our new identity in Christ. As we walk in obedience to God's Word and surrender to His work in us, we experience ongoing transformation into the likeness of Christ.

How can we keep the new person spiritually strong?

Maintaining spiritual strength as the new person in Christ is essential for our growth and perseverance in the faith. It requires intentional practices and a reliance on God's grace and power. The Scriptures provide guidance on how we can keep the new person spiritually strong.

Scriptural Support:

- 1 Peter 2:2 (ESV): "Like newborn infants, long for the pure spiritual milk, that by it you may grow up into salvation."
- Colossians 3:16 (ESV): "Let the word of Christ dwell in you richly, teaching and admonishing one another in all wisdom, singing psalms and hymns and spiritual songs, with thankfulness in your hearts to God."

Longing for Spiritual Nourishment

To keep the new person spiritually strong, we need to have a deep longing for spiritual nourishment. Just as newborn infants crave milk for their growth, we are to long for the pure spiritual milk of God's Word (1 Peter 2:2). This involves a hunger and thirst for God's truth, a desire to understand His Word, and a willingness to apply it to our lives. Regular study and meditation on Scripture, along with an attitude of humility and teachability, contribute to our spiritual growth and strength.

Letting the Word of Christ Dwell Richly

A vital aspect of maintaining spiritual strength is allowing the Word of Christ to dwell richly within us (Colossians 3:16). This means immersing ourselves in God's Word, allowing it to saturate our minds and hearts. By regularly reading, studying, and meditating on the Scriptures, we open ourselves to the transformative work of the Holy Spirit. The Word of God provides guidance, correction, encouragement, and nourishment for our spiritual lives. It shapes our thinking, informs our decisions, and helps us discern God's will. As we allow the Word to dwell richly in us, it strengthens our faith and empowers us to live in obedience to God's commands.

Fellowship and Worship

Maintaining spiritual strength also involves active participation in fellowship and worship within the community of believers. Colossians 3:16 encourages teaching and admonishing one another in all wisdom, singing psalms and hymns and spiritual songs, and expressing thankfulness in our hearts to God. Gathering with fellow believers, participating in worship, and engaging in mutual encouragement and accountability are vital for our spiritual well-being. The support and fellowship of other believers help us stay grounded in our faith and provide opportunities for growth, learning, and serving.

Prayer and Dependence on God's Spirit

Prayer is another essential component in keeping the new person spiritually strong. Through prayer, we communicate with God, seek His guidance, express our needs and desires, and offer thanksgiving and praise. Prayer deepens our relationship with God and helps us rely on His strength, wisdom, and grace. We also depend on the Holy Spirit, who indwells believers, to empower and guide us in our spiritual journey. Yielding to the Spirit's leading and relying on His power enable us to live in alignment with our new nature in Christ.

Continual Growth and Transformation

Keeping the new person spiritually strong is an ongoing process of growth and transformation. It requires a daily commitment to seek God, study His Word, engage in fellowship, and depend on the Holy Spirit. By cultivating these practices and relying on God's grace, we can experience spiritual strength, maturity, and a steadfast walk with Him.

Recognizing the Power of Thoughts

Proverbs 23:7 (ASV) tells us, "For as he thinketh within himself, so is he." This verse underscores the importance of our thoughts in shaping who we are. When our minds are filled with self-defeating thoughts, they can inhibit our growth, joy, and peace.

Identifying Negative Thought Patterns

One of the first steps in dealing with self-defeating thoughts is identifying them. Cognitive Behavioral Therapy (CBT) suggests that negative thinking typically falls into one of several categories like overgeneralization, jumping to conclusions, or personalization. Be aware of these patterns, note when they occur and what triggers them.

Renewing the Mind with the Word of God

We are commanded in Romans 12:2 (ESV), "Do not be conformed to this world, but be transformed by the renewal of your mind, that by testing you may discern what is the will of God, what is good and acceptable and perfect." One way to combat self-defeating thoughts is to immerse our minds in the Word of God. This allows His truth to reshape our thought patterns and perceptions.

Replacing Negative Thoughts with God's Truth

As you identify negative thoughts, actively replace them with God's truths found in the Bible. For instance, if you're feeling worthless, remember Genesis 1:27 (ASV), "And God created man in his own image, in the image of God created he him." Remember, our worth comes from being God's creation and bearing His image, not from worldly achievements or approval.

The Role of Prayer

Prayer is a powerful tool in dealing with self-defeating thoughts. Philippians 4:6-7 (ESV) instructs, "Do not be anxious about anything, but in everything by prayer and supplication with thanksgiving let your requests be made known to God. And the peace of God, which surpasses all understanding, will guard your hearts and your minds in Christ Jesus."

Cultivating Positive Thinking

Consider practicing cognitive reframing, a CBT technique that involves viewing situations from a different perspective. By focusing on God's blessings and promises, we can cultivate a mindset of gratitude and hope. As we learn in Philippians 4:8 (ESV), "Finally, brothers, whatever is true, whatever is honorable, whatever is just, whatever is pure, whatever is lovely, whatever is commendable, if there is any excellence, if there is anything worthy of praise, think about these things."

Biblical Counseling and Community Support

Seeking help from a Biblical counselor or a supportive Christian community can provide further help in dealing with self-defeating thoughts. Having others who can provide wise counsel, pray for you, and remind you of God's truths is invaluable. Proverbs 11:14 (ASV) states, "Where no wise guidance is, the people falleth: But in the multitude of counselors there is safety."

Relying on the Holy Spirit

The Holy Spirit plays a crucial role in renewing our minds and helping us overcome negative thoughts. Galatians 5:22-23 (ESV) assures, "But the fruit of the Spirit is love, joy, peace, patience, kindness, goodness, faithfulness, gentleness, self-control; against such things there is no law." By relying on the Holy Spirit, we can experience a deep-seated transformation in our thought life.

In conclusion, overcoming self-defeating thoughts is a process that requires self-awareness, active reliance on God's Word, the application of cognitive techniques, prayer, support from others, and the indwelling power of the Holy Spirit. It's a transformative journey that aligns our thoughts more closely with God's truths, liberating us from the bondage of negativity.

CHAPTER 7 What Is the Path to Behavioral Change?

Questions and Answers

What can result from a lack of self-control? Why do we need to discuss the subject of self-control? (Galatians 5:22-23)

A lack of self-control can have detrimental consequences in various aspects of our lives. When we allow our desires, emotions, or impulses to dictate our actions without restraint, it can lead to destructive behaviors and negative outcomes. The Scriptures provide insight into the consequences of lacking self-control.

Scriptural Support:

- Proverbs 25:28 (ESV): "A man without self-control is like a city broken into and left without walls."

- 2 Peter 1:5-7 (ESV): "For this very reason, make every effort to supplement your faith with virtue, and virtue with knowledge, and knowledge with self-control, and self-control with steadfastness, and steadfastness with godliness, and godliness with brotherly affection, and brotherly affection with love."

Broken Walls: Vulnerability and Chaos

Proverbs 25:28 compares a person without self-control to a city broken into and left without walls. In ancient times, city walls provided protection and security. Similarly, self-control acts as a safeguard, protecting us from harmful influences and impulsive actions. When we lack self-control, we become vulnerable to temptation, sinful behaviors, and the consequences that follow. It can lead to chaos, instability, and damage in our lives.

Spiritual Growth and Virtues

The need to discuss the subject of self-control arises from its significance in our spiritual growth and the development of other virtues. In 2 Peter 1:5-7, self-control is listed as one of the qualities to supplement our faith. It is part of the progression that leads to godliness, brotherly affection, and love. Self-control allows us to align our desires and actions with God's will, promoting righteousness and a Christ-like character.

Exercising Restraint and Discipline

Discussing self-control is crucial because it reminds us of the importance of restraining our impulses and desires within the boundaries of godly principles. It involves discipline and intentional choices to honor God and live according to His commands. Self-control empowers us to resist temptation, overcome sinful habits, and make wise decisions that align with our faith.

Seeking the Help of the Holy Spirit

Developing and maintaining self-control is a challenging task that requires reliance on the power of the Holy Spirit. We need the Holy Spirit's guidance and strength to overcome our natural inclinations and grow in self-control. Through prayer, seeking God's wisdom, and surrendering to the work of the Spirit in our lives, we can develop the fruit of self-control (Galatians 5:22-23).

Why do we need self-control?

Self-control plays a crucial role in our lives as believers. It is a virtue that enables us to align our thoughts, actions, and desires with God's will. The Scriptures provide insight into the reasons why self-control is essential for our spiritual well-being.

Scriptural Support:

- Proverbs 25:28 (ASV): "He that hath no rule over his own spirit is like a city that is broken down and without walls."

- 1 Corinthians 9:25 (ESV): "Every athlete exercises self-control in all things. They do it to receive a perishable wreath, but we an imperishable."

Guarding Our Spirit: Protection and Security

Proverbs 25:28 portrays a person without self-control as a city that is broken down and without walls. In ancient times, city walls served as a means of protection, shielding the inhabitants from external threats. Likewise, self-control acts as a protective barrier, guarding our spirit and preventing us from succumbing to temptations, sinful desires, and impulsive actions. It provides a sense of security and stability in our spiritual journey.

Achieving Spiritual Excellence: An Eternal Reward

1 Corinthians 9:25 draws a parallel between self-control and the discipline of athletes. Athletes exercise self-control in their training and competitions to obtain a perishable wreath or crown. Similarly, as followers of Christ, we are called to exercise self-control in all areas of our lives, not for a temporary reward but for an imperishable one. This eternal reward encompasses spiritual growth, a deepening relationship with God, and the inheritance of eternal life.

Honoring God: Living in Obedience

Self-control is vital because it enables us to live in obedience to God's commands and principles. It empowers us to resist temptation, overcome sinful habits, and make choices that align with God's standards. By exercising self-control, we demonstrate our love for God and our desire to honor Him in all aspects of our lives.

A Fruit of the Spirit: Empowered by the Holy Spirit

Self-control is not solely a product of our own willpower but is a fruit of the Holy Spirit working within us. As believers, we have the indwelling presence of the Holy Spirit who empowers and enables us to exercise self-control. Through our dependence on the Spirit, we can grow in self-control and live according to God's purposes.

What should be encouraging to any who are struggling to control their wrong desires? (1 Kings 8:46-50)

Encouragement for Those Struggling to Control Wrong Desires

Struggling with wrong desires and sinful tendencies can be disheartening and challenging. However, the Scriptures offer encouragement and hope to all who are in this battle. One such passage that provides comfort and encouragement is found in 1 Kings 8:46-50.

Scripture: 1 Kings 8:46-50 (ASV)

"And if they sin against thee (for there is no man that sinneth not), and thou be angry with them, and deliver them to the enemy, so that they carry them away captive unto the land of the enemy, far off or near; yet if they shall bethink themselves in the land whither they are carried captive, and turn again, and make supplication unto thee in the land of them that carried them captive, saying, We have sinned, and have done perversely, we have dealt wickedly; if they return unto thee with all their heart and with all their soul in the land of their enemies, who carried them captive, and pray unto thee toward their land, which thou gavest unto their fathers, the city which thou hast chosen, and the house which I have built for thy name; then hear thou their prayer and their supplication in heaven thy dwelling-place, and maintain their cause, and forgive thy people who have sinned against thee, and all their transgressions wherein they have transgressed against thee; and give them compassion before those who carried them captive, that they may have compassion on them."

Acknowledging Sin and Seeking God's Forgiveness

The passage reminds us that all human beings, without exception, are prone to sin. It recognizes the reality of human fallibility and the struggles we face in controlling wrong desires. It acknowledges that at times, our sins may lead us into captivity and separation from God. However, there is hope for those who sincerely repent and turn back to God.

Bethinking Oneself and Turning to God

The passage encourages individuals to "bethink themselves" or reflect upon their actions while in captivity and turn back to God with repentance. It highlights the importance of recognizing and admitting our sins, acknowledging our perverseness and wickedness. It is a call to genuine self-reflection and a turning of the heart and soul toward God.

Prayer and Supplication

The passage emphasizes the power of prayer and supplication as a means of seeking forgiveness and reconciliation with God. It describes the posture of the repentant heart, praying toward the land of promise and the dwelling place of God. It is a plea for God's mercy and forgiveness, recognizing His authority to grant compassion and restoration.

God's Response: Forgiveness and Compassion

The passage assures that when the repentant sinner sincerely seeks God with all their heart and soul, God hears their prayer and supplication. He responds with forgiveness, maintaining their cause, and granting them compassion before those who held them captive. It reveals God's gracious and merciful nature, willing to restore and show compassion to those who humbly seek Him.

Encouragement for Those Struggling

This passage serves as an encouragement to all who are struggling to control their wrong desires and tendencies. It reassures them that even in their captivity and separation from God, there is a way of repentance, forgiveness, and restoration. It highlights the importance of genuine self-reflection, turning to God with all their heart and soul, and seeking His forgiveness through prayer and supplication. It reminds them of God's compassion and willingness to hear their cries for help.

What example of self-control does God set for us? (Deuteronomy 32:4; Exodus 34:6; Job 2:2-6)

God's Example of Self-Control

As our perfect and righteous Creator, God sets the ultimate example of self-control for us to follow. Through various Scriptures, we can gain insights into God's character and His display of self-control.

Scripture: Deuteronomy 32:4 (ASV)

"The Rock, his work is perfect; for all his ways are justice: a God of faithfulness and without iniquity, just and right is he."

Scripture: Exodus 34:6 (ASV)

"And Jehovah passed by before him, and proclaimed, Jehovah, Jehovah, a God merciful and gracious, slow to anger, and abundant in lovingkindness and truth."

Scripture: Job 2:2-6 (ASV)

"And Jehovah said unto Satan, From whence comest thou? And Satan answered Jehovah, and said, From going to and fro in the earth, and from walking up and down in it. And Jehovah said unto Satan, Hast thou considered my servant Job? for there is none like him in the earth, a perfect and an upright man, one that feareth God, and turneth away from evil: and he still holdeth fast his integrity, although thou movedst me against him, to destroy him without cause. And Satan answered Jehovah, and said, Skin for skin, yea, all that a man hath will he give for his life. But put forth thy hand now, and touch his bone and his flesh, and he will renounce thee to thy face."

Perfect and Just in His Ways

Deuteronomy 32:4 declares that God's work is perfect, and all His ways are just. This speaks of His flawless nature and the perfect execution of His plans. God's self-control is evident in His consistent adherence to justice and righteousness. He does not act impulsively or recklessly but remains steadfast and controlled in His judgments and actions.

Merciful, Gracious, and Slow to Anger

Exodus 34:6 describes God's character as merciful, gracious, and slow to anger. Despite the rebellion and sin of humanity, God demonstrates incredible self-control by extending mercy and grace instead of immediate judgment. His patience and forbearance reflect His ability to control His anger and act according to His loving and compassionate nature.

Job's Example of Integrity

In the book of Job, we witness God's affirmation of Job's integrity and self-control. Job remains steadfast and faithful to God even amidst immense suffering and Satan's challenges. Job's commitment to righteousness and refusal to renounce God demonstrates his extraordinary self-control and unwavering trust in the midst of trials.

Implications for Our Lives

God's example of self-control calls us to emulate His character in our own lives. We are encouraged to strive for perfection, righteousness, and integrity, relying on God's strength to exercise self-control in our thoughts, words, and actions. By imitating God's self-control, we can resist temptation, act justly, extend mercy, and exhibit patience in our relationships and interactions with others. Ultimately, God's example serves as an inspiration and guide for us to grow in self-control and reflect His character to the world around us.

What can we learn from God's example? (Psalm 141:3; Proverbs 14:29; 15:28; 19:2)

Lessons from God's Example

By examining several Scriptures, we can gain valuable insights from God's example and apply them to our lives.

Scripture: Psalm 141:3 (ASV)

"Set a watch, O Jehovah, before my mouth; keep the door of my lips."

Scripture: Proverbs 14:29 (ASV)

"He that is slow to anger is of great understanding; but he that is hasty of spirit exalteth folly."

Scripture: Proverbs 15:28 (ASV)

"The heart of the righteous studieth to answer; but the mouth of the wicked poureth out evil things."

Scripture: Proverbs 19:2 (ASV)

"Desire without knowledge is not good; and he that hasteth with his feet sinneth."

Guarding Our Speech

Psalm 141:3 reminds us of the importance of controlling our words. Like David, we should ask God to set a guard over our mouths and keep watch over what we speak. God's example teaches us the significance of using our words wisely, refraining from gossip, slander, and harmful speech.

Exercising Patience and Understanding

Proverbs 14:29 highlights the virtue of being slow to anger. Just as God displays self-control in His patience, we are encouraged to cultivate understanding and resist hasty reactions that can lead to foolishness. Learning from God's example, we strive to respond to situations with calmness and wisdom rather than allowing our emotions to dictate our actions.

Thoughtful Responses and Seeking Knowledge

Proverbs 15:28 emphasizes the importance of a righteous heart that carefully considers its responses. God's example teaches us to study and seek understanding before speaking. Instead of hastily pouring out evil or hurtful words, we should emulate God's self-control by responding thoughtfully, with kindness, and with an attitude of seeking knowledge and wisdom.

Avoiding Impulsive Actions

Proverbs 19:2 cautions against acting on desires without proper knowledge. God's example demonstrates self-control in His actions, and we are encouraged to follow suit. Rushing into decisions or actions without careful consideration can lead to sin and negative consequences. Learning from God's example, we exercise self-control by aligning our actions with wisdom, knowledge, and a deep understanding of God's principles.

Implications for Our Lives

The lessons derived from God's example of self-control call us to examine our own behavior and align it with His righteous character. We should guard our speech, exercise patience and understanding, respond thoughtfully, seek knowledge, and avoid impulsive actions. By reflecting God's self-control, we bring honor to His name, promote peace in our relationships, and cultivate a life that is pleasing to Him. Emulating God's example enables us to grow in spiritual maturity, positively influence others, and live in accordance with His will.

Where can we find good examples of self-control? What helped Joseph to resist temptation when Potiphar's wife tried to seduce him? (Genesis 39:6, 9; Proverbs 1:10)

Sources of Good Examples of Self-Control

The Bible provides us with numerous examples of individuals who demonstrated self-control in the face of temptation or challenging circumstances. These examples serve as sources of inspiration and guidance for us to develop and strengthen our own self-control.

Joseph's Example of Resisting Temptation
Scripture: Genesis 39:6 (ASV)

"So he left all that he had in Joseph's hand, and he knew not aught that was with him, save the bread which he did eat. And Joseph was comely, and well-favored."

Scripture: Genesis 39:9 (ASV)

"[Joseph said to Potiphar's wife] how then can I do this great wickedness, and sin against God?"

Scripture: Proverbs 1:10 (ASV)

"My son, if sinners entice thee, consent thou not."

Joseph's story in Genesis 39 provides a powerful example of self-control. When faced with the advances of Potiphar's wife, Joseph resisted temptation and maintained his integrity. Despite being in a vulnerable position, he remained faithful to both Potiphar, his master, and to God.

Joseph's ability to resist temptation can be attributed to his strong sense of morality, his fear of sinning against God, and his commitment to doing what is right. He recognized the gravity of the situation and firmly refused to engage in sinful behavior.

Implications for Our Lives

Joseph's example teaches us the importance of honoring our commitments, maintaining moral integrity, and standing firm against temptation. We can draw strength from his story when facing our own trials, whether they involve moral dilemmas, sexual temptation, or other forms of pressure.

Additionally, Proverbs 1:10 provides general wisdom about not yielding to the influence of sinners. It encourages us to exercise self-control and refuse to give in to negative influences or peer pressure.

By studying Joseph's example and heeding the wisdom found in Proverbs, we can develop and strengthen our own self-control. We learn to prioritize our relationship with God, maintain moral purity, and resist temptations that could lead us astray from His path. Through prayer, seeking wisdom, and relying on the Holy Spirit, we can cultivate self-control and emulate the righteousness and integrity demonstrated by Joseph.

How can you prepare yourself to resist temptations? (Psalm 26:4, 5; Proverbs 22:3)

Preparing Yourself to Resist Temptations

To resist temptations and strengthen your ability to exercise self-control, the Bible provides guidance and wisdom on how to prepare yourself mentally, spiritually, and practically.

Scripture: Psalm 26:4, 5 (ASV)

"I have not sat with men of falsehood; neither will I go in with dissemblers. I hate the assembly of evil-doers, and will not sit with the wicked."

Scripture: Proverbs 22:3 (ASV)

"The prudent seeth the evil, and hideth himself; but the simple pass on, and suffer for it."

Avoiding Unrighteous Associations

Psalm 26:4, 5 emphasizes the importance of avoiding the company of those who engage in falsehood and wickedness. By consciously choosing not to associate with individuals who promote or engage in unrighteousness, we create a protective boundary that helps safeguard our hearts and minds from being influenced by their negative behaviors and temptations. Surrounding ourselves with people of integrity and godly character can strengthen our resolve to resist temptations.

Being Prudent and Foreseeing Evil

Proverbs 22:3 highlights the significance of being prudent and having foresight. Being prudent means being cautious, wise, and discerning. By actively observing and recognizing potential sources of temptation or situations that can lead us astray, we can take proactive steps to avoid them. This may involve setting boundaries, establishing accountability, or making decisions that prioritize righteousness and holiness.

Implications for Our Lives

To prepare ourselves to resist temptations effectively, we can:

1. **Choose our associations wisely**: Surround ourselves with individuals who share our commitment to godliness and righteousness, avoiding the company of those who engage in unrighteousness.

2. **Stay vigilant and discerning**: Develop a discerning spirit that recognizes potential sources of temptation and sinful influences. This awareness enables us to take preventive measures to safeguard ourselves from falling into temptation.

3. **Set clear boundaries**: Establish personal boundaries and guidelines that help us avoid compromising situations and protect us from being drawn into sinful behavior.

4. **Seek accountability**: Engage in relationships with trusted individuals who can provide support, encouragement, and accountability in our journey to resist temptations. This can be a mentor, a spiritual advisor, or a trusted friend who shares our commitment to righteousness.

By incorporating these principles into our lives, relying on the guidance of the Holy Spirit, and drawing strength from prayer and the study of God's Word, we can better prepare ourselves to resist temptations and exercise self-control.

What happens to many young ones at school? What can help young Christians to resist the temptation to break God's laws? (2 Timothy 2:22; Proverbs 7; 2 Samuel 13:1, 2, 10-15, 28-32)

Challenges Young Ones Face at School

Many young ones face various challenges at school, including the temptation to break God's laws. Schools can be environments where peer pressure, worldly influences, and moral compromises are prevalent. The Bible provides guidance on how young Christians can resist these temptations and remain faithful to God's standards.

Scripture: 2 Timothy 2:22 (ASV)

"**Flee youthful passions and pursue righteousness, faith, love, and peace**, along with those who call on the Lord from a pure heart."

Scripture: Proverbs 7 (ASV)

Proverbs 7 narrates a cautionary tale of a young man who falls into the temptation of an immoral woman. This story serves as a warning against the allure of sexual immorality and the consequences it brings.

Scripture: 2 Samuel 13:1, 2, 10-15, 28-32 (ASV)

The story of Amnon and Tamar in 2 Samuel 13 highlights the tragic consequences of yielding to lustful desires and failing to control them. It serves as a sobering reminder of the destructive consequences of indulging in immoral behavior.

Resisting Temptation and Upholding God's Laws

To help young Christians resist the temptation to break God's laws, the following principles and actions are encouraged:

1. **Flee from youthful passions**: Young ones are advised to **avoid situations, influences, and relationships that can lead them astray**. Instead, they should actively pursue righteousness, faith, love, and peace, seeking companionship with those who share a genuine devotion to God.

2. **Develop discernment and wisdom**: The story in Proverbs 7 teaches young ones to **exercise discernment and wisdom** when faced with temptations. They should be vigilant and aware of the deceitful tactics used to entice them into sinful behavior. By staying rooted in God's Word, they can discern right from wrong and make wise choices.

3. **Seek guidance and accountability**: Young ones should **seek guidance from mature Christians**, whether parents, elders, or spiritual mentors. Having someone to provide guidance, support, and accountability can help them navigate the challenges they face.

4. **Understand the consequences**: Reflecting on the tragic accounts like that of Amnon and Tamar serves as a **reminder of the destructive consequences** that come from giving in to temptations and violating God's laws. It encourages young ones to consider the long-term effects of their actions and the importance of upholding God's standards.

By embracing these principles, young Christians can resist the pressures and temptations they encounter at school. Through prayer, reliance on God's guidance, and the support of fellow believers, they can develop a strong foundation of faith and self-control that enables them to make choices in harmony with God's will.

How did Joseph control his feelings toward his brothers? In what situations do we have to control our feelings? (Genesis 43:30, 31; 45:1; Proverbs 16:32; 17:27)

Joseph's Control of His Feelings

Joseph provides an excellent example of self-control and emotional restraint in his interactions with his brothers. Despite the mistreatment he endured at their hands, Joseph displayed remarkable self-control and managed his emotions wisely.

Scripture: Genesis 43:30-31 (ASV)

"**And Joseph made haste; for his heart yearned over his brother**: and he sought where to weep; and he entered into his chamber, and wept there. And he washed his face, and came out; and he refrained himself, and said, Set on bread."

Joseph, upon seeing his brother Benjamin, felt intense emotions of love and compassion. However, he controlled his feelings, refrained from openly expressing them, and chose to maintain composure in the situation.

Scripture: Genesis 45:1 (ASV)

"**Then Joseph could not refrain himself before all them that stood by him**; and he cried, Cause every man to go out from me. And there stood no man with him, while Joseph made himself known unto his brethren."

Although Joseph initially controlled his emotions, there came a point where he could no longer contain himself. In this instance, he showed great self-control by purposefully dismissing all other witnesses before revealing his identity to his brothers.

Situations Requiring Emotional Control

The Bible teaches that self-control is crucial in various situations. Here are a few examples:

1. **Provoking situations**: Proverbs 16:32 (ASV) states, "**He that is slow to anger is better than the mighty; and he that ruleth his spirit than he that taketh a city.**" Controlling our anger and maintaining a calm spirit, even when provoked, demonstrates strength and wisdom.

2. **Wise communication**: Proverbs 17:27 (ASV) says, "**He that spareth his words hath knowledge: and he that is of a cool spirit is a man of understanding.**" Exercising self-control over our words and emotions during conversations helps to avoid unnecessary conflicts and promotes understanding.

3. **Resisting temptation**: Throughout the Bible, believers are encouraged to exercise self-control in resisting various temptations, such as immoral desires, dishonesty, or destructive behaviors. This self-control enables us to align our actions with God's commands.

In these situations and many others, self-control is necessary to maintain peace, promote healthy relationships, and honor God's standards. By following the example of Joseph and relying on the guidance of God's Word, we can develop the discipline to manage our emotions and respond with wisdom and self-control.

What lessons can we learn from events in King David's life? (1 Samuel 26:9-11; 2 Samuel 16:5-10 1 Samuel 25:10-13; 2 Samuel 11:2-4; 1 Corinthians 10:12)

Lessons from King David's Life

The life of King David, as recorded in the Bible, provides valuable lessons and insights for believers. Here are a few key events from David's life and the lessons we can learn from them:

1. David's Mercy and Self-Control: In 1 Samuel 26:9-11 (ASV), we see an example of David sparing the life of King Saul, who was seeking to kill him: **"And David said to Abishai, Destroy him not; for who can put forth his hand against Jehovah's anointed, and be guiltless?... Jehovah forbid that I should put forth my hand against Jehovah's anointed..."** Despite having an opportunity to take revenge, David chose mercy and exercised self-control by refusing to harm Saul. This teaches us the importance of showing grace, forgiveness, and self-restraint in dealing with our enemies or those who wrong us.

2. Responding to Insults with Grace: In 2 Samuel 16:5-10 (ASV), David faced insults and cursing from Shimei. Instead of reacting with anger or seeking vengeance, David responded with humility and entrusted the situation to God, saying, **"So let him curse, because Jehovah hath said unto him, Curse David."** This teaches us the value of responding to insults or mistreatment with grace, leaving justice in God's hands and not retaliating in kind.

3. Nabal's Insult and David's Restraint: In 1 Samuel 25:10-13 (ASV), David was insulted by Nabal, a wealthy man who refused to offer him and his men provisions. Despite feeling disrespected, David chose not to retaliate and exercised self-control. This event reminds us to respond wisely when faced with offenses or disrespect, avoiding impulsive reactions and seeking peaceful resolutions instead.

4. David's Adultery with Bathsheba: In 2 Samuel 11:2-4 (ASV), David succumbed to temptation and committed adultery with Bathsheba, the wife of Uriah. This grave sin highlights the consequences of yielding to sinful desires and the destructive path it can lead to. It serves as a warning about the importance of guarding our hearts, resisting temptation, and seeking God's help to overcome sinful urges.

5. Lessons from David's Life - 1 Corinthians 10:12 (ESV): In 1 Corinthians 10:12, the apostle Paul provides a general lesson for all believers based on the experiences of the Israelites, including David: **"Therefore let anyone who thinks that he stands take heed lest he fall."** This verse reminds us to be humble and vigilant, recognizing our own vulnerability to temptation and sin. It cautions us against complacency and encourages us to rely on God's strength rather than relying on our own abilities.

These events from King David's life demonstrate the importance of self-control, mercy, grace, humility, and reliance on God's guidance. By studying and reflecting on these lessons, we can gain wisdom and apply them to our own lives, seeking to walk in obedience and righteousness before God.

How can Bible study help you and your family to develop self-control? (Joshua 1:8; Romans 15:4; James 1:5)

The Benefits of Bible Study for Developing Self-Control

Bible study plays a vital role in helping individuals and families develop self-control. Here are some ways in which engaging in Bible study can assist in cultivating self-control, along with relevant Scriptures:

1. Guided by God's Word - Joshua 1:8 (ASV): In Joshua 1:8, God instructs Joshua: **"This book of the law shall not depart out of thy mouth, but thou shalt meditate thereon day and night, that thou mayest observe to do according to all that is written therein:**

for then thou shalt make thy way prosperous, and then thou shalt have good success." Regular study and meditation on God's Word provide guidance and direction for our lives. By immersing ourselves in Scripture, we gain wisdom, understanding, and the principles needed to exercise self-control in various situations.

2. Learning from Examples - Romans 15:4 (ESV): Romans 15:4 reminds us of the value of the Old Testament narratives and examples: **"For whatever was written in former days was written for our instruction, that through endurance and through the encouragement of the Scriptures we might have hope."** Studying the accounts of individuals in the Bible, their triumphs, and their failures, helps us learn valuable lessons. By examining their experiences and the consequences of their actions, we can gain insights into the importance of self-control and the potential pitfalls of giving in to temptation.

3. Seeking Wisdom and Guidance - James 1:5 (ASV): James 1:5 encourages us to seek God's wisdom: **"But if any of you lacks wisdom, let him ask of God, who giveth to all liberally and upbraideth not; and it shall be given him."** Through Bible study, we have access to the wisdom of God. As we delve into His Word, we can pray for understanding and guidance, asking for the discernment needed to exercise self-control in challenging situations.

4. Nurturing Faith and Renewing the Mind: Bible study nurtures our faith and contributes to the renewal of our minds. It helps us align our thoughts, attitudes, and behaviors with God's truth. By immersing ourselves in Scripture regularly, we reinforce the values of self-control and develop a renewed mindset that is in harmony with God's will.

5. Applying God's Principles: As we study the Bible, we encounter principles and teachings that provide practical guidance for self-control. These include principles of love, forgiveness, patience, humility, and moderation. By studying and internalizing these principles, we equip ourselves with the tools needed to exercise self-control in all areas of life.

Engaging in regular Bible study, individually and as a family, fosters spiritual growth and provides a solid foundation for developing self-control. It helps us understand God's will, learn from biblical examples, seek wisdom, nurture our faith, renew our minds, and apply God's principles in our daily lives. Through this ongoing study and application of Scripture, we are empowered to resist temptation, make wise choices, and exhibit self-control in all circumstances.

In what ways can parents help their children to develop self-control? (Proverbs 1:5, 7, 8)

Parental Guidance for Developing Self-Control in Children

Parents play a crucial role in helping their children develop self-control. Here are some ways in which parents can assist their children in cultivating this important virtue, along with relevant Scriptures:

1. Teach Wisdom and Understanding - Proverbs 1:5 (ASV): Proverbs 1:5 states: "**That the wise man may hear, and increase in learning; and that the man of understanding may attain unto sound counsels.**" Parents can impart wisdom and understanding to their children by teaching them the principles and values found in God's Word. By instructing them in the ways of righteousness, parents provide a foundation for developing self-control.

2. Emphasize the Fear of the Lord - Proverbs 1:7 (ASV): Proverbs 1:7 declares: "**The fear of Jehovah is the beginning of knowledge; But the foolish despise wisdom and instruction.**" Parents can instill in their children a reverence and respect for God, teaching them that living in accordance with His wisdom leads to true understanding and self-control. By emphasizing the importance of a God-centered life, parents lay the groundwork for developing self-control rooted in a relationship with God.

3. Provide Loving Discipline - Proverbs 1:8 (ASV): Proverbs 1:8 advises: "**My son, hear the instruction of thy father, And forsake not the law of thy mother.**" Parents can provide loving discipline by setting clear boundaries and expectations for their children. This includes teaching them self-control through consistent guidance and correction. By enforcing appropriate consequences for misbehavior and encouraging positive behavior, parents help their children develop self-discipline and self-regulation.

4. Model Self-Control: Parents serve as powerful role models for their children. By exhibiting self-control in their own words, actions, and attitudes, parents demonstrate the importance of this virtue. Children learn by observing and imitating their parents, so it is crucial for parents to model self-control in various situations and challenges they face. This consistent example reinforces the value of self-control and encourages children to follow suit.

5. Cultivate Open Communication: Creating an atmosphere of open communication within the family allows parents to teach and guide their children effectively. By maintaining open lines of dialogue, parents can discuss the importance of self-control, share biblical principles, and address any challenges or questions their children may have. Encouraging children to express their thoughts and feelings while providing loving guidance helps them develop self-awareness and the ability to make wise choices.

By incorporating these principles into their parenting approach, parents can actively contribute to their children's development of self-control. Teaching wisdom, emphasizing the fear of the Lord, providing loving discipline, modeling self-control, and fostering open communication create a supportive environment for children to grow in this important virtue. Through consistent guidance, parents can help their children navigate challenges, resist temptations, and develop self-control that is rooted in a deep understanding of God's Word.

Why do we need to choose our friends wisely? (Proverbs 13:20)

Choosing Friends Wisely: The Importance of Selecting Companions

The Bible provides wisdom regarding the significance of choosing our friends wisely. Here is a closer look at the reasons why we need to exercise discernment in our choice of companions, as supported by Proverbs 13:20 (ASV):

Proverbs 13:20 (ASV): "He that walketh with wise men shall be wise; But the companion of fools shall smart for it."

1. Influence and Association: The people we associate with have a significant impact on our lives. Proverbs 13:20 teaches that walking with wise individuals leads to wisdom, while being a companion of fools brings harm. The company we keep can shape our attitudes, beliefs, and behavior. Therefore, choosing friends who exhibit wisdom and godly character can positively influence our own development.

2. Learning and Growth: Walking with wise individuals provides an opportunity for learning and growth. When we surround ourselves with wise friends who possess understanding and discernment, we have the privilege of gaining knowledge and insight from their experiences and perspectives. Engaging in meaningful conversations, sharing wisdom, and receiving counsel from wise companions can contribute to our personal development and spiritual growth.

3. Accountability and Support: Choosing friends wisely ensures that we have individuals who hold us accountable and provide support in our journey of faith. Wise friends can offer encouragement, correction, and guidance, helping us stay on the right path and avoid harmful choices. Their presence strengthens our resolve to make righteous decisions, exercise self-control, and live according to God's principles.

4. Protection and Avoiding Harm: Proverbs 13:20 warns of the consequences of being a companion of fools. Associating with individuals who lack wisdom and godly values can expose us to harmful influences and lead us astray. Choosing friends who align with godly principles protects us from compromising our faith and helps us avoid the negative consequences that can arise from unwise associations.

5. Reflecting God's Character: By choosing wise companions, we reflect the character of God and fulfill His desire for us to live in wisdom and righteousness. As followers of Christ, we are called to surround ourselves with like-minded believers who can encourage us in our faith journey. By choosing friends who demonstrate godly virtues, we manifest God's wisdom and love to the world and contribute to the building of a strong community of believers.

Understanding the Need for Change

The first step toward behavioral change is recognizing the need for change. We see a powerful example of this in the Bible when King David acknowledged his sin with Bathsheba in Psalm 51:3-4 (ESV), "For I know my transgressions, and my sin is ever before me. Against you, you only, have I sinned and done what is evil in your sight." The conviction to change our behaviors often arises from an understanding that our actions have displeased God and hurt others.

The Role of Repentance

Repentance is a crucial element of biblical behavioral change. This involves not just feeling sorry about our actions, but also making a conscious decision to turn away from them. Ezekiel 18:30-31 (ASV) declares, "Repent, and turn yourselves from all your transgressions; so iniquity shall not be your ruin. Cast away from you all your transgressions, wherein ye have transgressed; and make you a new heart and a new spirit."

Adopting New Behaviors

Changing behavior involves replacing old, harmful habits with new, healthy ones. Romans 12:21 (ESV) states, "Do not be overcome by evil, but overcome evil with good." Here, Paul not only encourages us to refrain from evil actions but to actively pursue good actions. Consider seeking guidance from a Christian counselor to help identify positive behaviors that align with your faith and values.

The Power of God's Word

Immersing ourselves in God's Word is instrumental in behavioral change. The Word of God is living and active, and it can penetrate our hearts and minds to prompt change. Psalm 119:11 (ASV) attests, "Thy word have I laid up in my heart, That I might not sin against thee."

Involvement of Community

The Christian community can provide support, accountability, and encouragement as we pursue behavioral change. Hebrews 10:24-25 (ESV) instructs, "And let us consider how to stir up one another to love and good works, not neglecting to meet together, as is the habit of some, but encouraging one another."

Prayer and Dependence on God

Biblical behavioral change is not just a human endeavor—it requires divine intervention. Regularly pray for God's guidance and strength in your journey. Remember Philippians 4:6-7 (ESV), "Do not be anxious about anything, but in everything by prayer and supplication with thanksgiving let your requests be made known to God."

Embracing the Process

Biblical behavioral change is a process, not an event. It takes time, patience, and perseverance. Galatians 6:9 (ASV) reassures, "And let us not be weary in well-doing: for in due season we shall reap, if we faint not."

Relying on the Holy Spirit

The Holy Spirit plays a vital role in our journey towards behavioral change. It is the Spirit that convicts us of sin, leads us to truth, and empowers us to live according to God's will. Romans 8:13 (ESV) says,

"For if you live according to the flesh you will die, but if by the Spirit you put to death the deeds of the body, you will live."

In conclusion, the path to biblical behavioral change involves understanding the need for change, repenting, adopting new behaviors, immersing ourselves in God's Word, leaning on the Christian community, regular prayer, embracing the process, and relying on the Holy Spirit. It is a transformative journey that brings us closer to Christ-likeness.

CHAPTER 8 How Do You Get Control Over Anger?

Questions and Answer

Why are people in the world today so angry? (James 4:1-2; Galatians 5:19-21; Ephesians 4:26-27; Romans 3:23; Proverbs 29:22; Colossians 3:13)

Understanding Anger in the World Today: Insights from Scripture

Anger is a prevalent emotion in the world today, and the Bible provides valuable insights into why people experience such strong feelings of anger. Let's explore relevant scriptures that shed light on this issue:

1. James 4:1-2 (ESV): "What causes quarrels and what causes fights among you? Is it not this, that your passions are at war within you? You desire and do not have, so you murder. You covet and cannot obtain, so you fight and quarrel."

James identifies the root cause of conflicts and fights among people: the inner desires and passions that are at war within them. When individuals crave things they cannot have or harbor selfish ambitions, it leads to resentment and contention, fueling anger and discord.

2. Galatians 5:19-21 (ESV): "Now the works of the flesh are evident: sexual immorality, impurity, sensuality, idolatry, sorcery, enmity, strife, jealousy, fits of anger, rivalries, dissensions, divisions, envy, drunkenness, orgies, and things like these."

Paul lists fits of anger as one of the works of the flesh, emphasizing its destructive nature. When people indulge in sinful behaviors and attitudes, it can give rise to anger and contribute to the overall climate of anger in society.

3. Ephesians 4:26-27 (ESV): "Be angry and do not sin; do not let the sun go down on your anger, and give no opportunity to the devil."

While anger itself is not inherently sinful, it can lead to sin if not properly managed. Paul advises believers to handle their anger in a righteous manner, not allowing it to fester or give the devil an opportunity to sow discord and division.

4. Romans 3:23 (ASV): "For all have sinned and fall short of the glory of God."

The fallen nature of humanity is a fundamental reason why people experience anger. Sin separates individuals from the perfect standard of God's glory, resulting in broken relationships, unmet expectations, and the eruption of anger.

5. Proverbs 29:22 (ASV): "An angry man stirreth up strife, and a wrathful man aboundeth in transgression."

The book of Proverbs highlights the consequences of unchecked anger, emphasizing how it stirs up conflicts and leads to further wrongdoing. Uncontrolled anger can escalate into a pattern of transgressions and harmful behavior.

6. Colossians 3:13 (ESV): "Bearing with one another and, if one has a complaint against another, forgiving each other; as the Lord has forgiven you, so you also must forgive."

Forgiveness is a powerful antidote to anger. When individuals cultivate a spirit of forgiveness, they break the cycle of anger and allow for reconciliation and healing. Choosing forgiveness aligns with God's example of extending His forgiveness to us, promoting peace and harmony.

In summary, the Bible identifies various factors contributing to the prevalence of anger in the world today. Inner desires, sinful behavior, unresolved conflicts, the fallen nature of humanity, and a lack of forgiveness can all fuel anger. However, Scripture provides guidance on managing anger, seeking reconciliation, and cultivating virtues that counteract its destructive effects. By following biblical principles, individuals can strive to address and mitigate anger, fostering a more peaceful and loving environment in their relationships and communities.

What Bible examples show the consequences of controlling or not controlling anger? (1 Corinthians 6:9-10; Ps. 32:5; Jas. 5:14; 1 Cor. 5:12; Acts 3:19)

Consequences of Controlling or Not Controlling Anger: Biblical Examples

The Bible provides numerous examples that demonstrate the consequences of either controlling or failing to control anger. These accounts serve as valuable lessons for understanding the impact of anger on individuals and their relationships. Let's explore some relevant scriptures:

1. 1 Corinthians 6:9-10 (ESV): "Do you not know that the unrighteous will not inherit the kingdom of God? Do not be deceived: neither the sexually immoral, nor idolaters, nor adulterers, nor men who practice homosexuality, nor thieves, nor the greedy, nor drunkards, nor revilers, nor swindlers will inherit the kingdom of God."

In this passage, Paul highlights various sinful behaviors that include uncontrolled anger. While not explicitly mentioned, the inclusion of "revilers" can encompass those who indulge in uncontrolled outbursts of anger. The consequences of uncontrolled anger, along with other sins, is the exclusion from inheriting the kingdom of God.

2. Psalm 32:5 (ASV): "I acknowledged my sin unto thee, and mine iniquity did I not hide: I said, I will confess my transgressions unto Jehovah; and thou forgavest the iniquity of my sin."

This verse expresses the consequences of failing to control anger and harboring it within. The psalmist acknowledges the destructive nature of unconfessed sin and experiences the forgiveness of God when taking responsibility for their actions, including uncontrolled anger.

3. James 5:14 (ESV): "Is anyone among you sick? Let him call for the elders of the church, and let them pray over him, anointing him with oil in the name of the Lord."

While not directly addressing the consequences of anger, this verse provides guidance on seeking healing and restoration within the context of a faith community. Uncontrolled anger can lead to broken relationships, emotional distress, and even physical ailments. Seeking support and prayer can help individuals find healing from the consequences of uncontrolled anger.

4. 1 Corinthians 5:12 (ESV): "For what have I to do with judging outsiders? Is it not those inside the church whom you are to judge?"

This verse speaks to the consequences of uncontrolled anger in the context of judgment and conflict within the church community. Unresolved anger can lead to division and strife, hindering the unity and effectiveness of the body of Christ.

5. Acts 3:19 (ESV): "Repent therefore, and turn again, that your sins may be blotted out."

This verse highlights the consequences of uncontrolled anger as a sin that requires repentance. Failing to address and control anger can lead to the accumulation of sins, which hinder one's relationship with God and others. Repentance and turning away from uncontrolled anger allow for the forgiveness and restoration of a right relationship with God.

These examples illustrate the consequences of uncontrolled anger, including exclusion from the kingdom of God, the need for confession and forgiveness, hindrance in community relationships, and the importance of repentance. On the other hand, practicing self-control over anger can lead to peace, reconciliation, and the preservation of relationships. Through these accounts, the Bible provides valuable lessons on the consequences of controlling or failing to control anger, urging individuals to pursue a righteous and self-controlled approach to their emotions.

How should we react if a fellow Christian hurts us? (Matt. 18:23-35; Ps. 103:9; Matt. 5:7; Jas. 2:13; Matthew 6:14-15; Job 42:8-10; Ephesians 4:31-32; Prov. 14:30; 11:17; Romans 12:19-21)

How to React If a Fellow Christian Hurts Us

When we experience hurt from a fellow Christian, the Bible provides guidance on how to respond in a way that promotes forgiveness, reconciliation, and restoration of relationships. Let's explore the relevant scriptures:

1. Matthew 18:23-35 (ESV): The Parable of the Unforgiving Servant This parable emphasizes the importance of forgiving others as God has forgiven us. The servant who received forgiveness from his master but refused to forgive a fellow servant faced severe consequences. It teaches us the necessity of extending forgiveness and showing mercy to those who have hurt us.

2. Psalm 103:9 (ASV) "He will not always chide; neither will he keep his anger forever."

This verse reminds us of God's merciful and forgiving nature. It encourages us to follow His example by not holding onto anger or grudges when someone hurts us, but rather to extend forgiveness and seek reconciliation.

3. Matthew 5:7 (ESV): The Beatitudes "Blessed are the merciful, for they shall receive mercy."

Jesus teaches the value of showing mercy to others. When we experience hurt, responding with mercy and compassion, even toward those who have hurt us, allows us to receive God's mercy and helps foster reconciliation.

4. James 2:13 (ESV) "For judgment is without mercy to one who has shown no mercy. Mercy triumphs over judgment."

This verse highlights the principle that showing mercy is more important than passing judgment. When we have been hurt, extending mercy to others instead of seeking revenge or holding grudges aligns with God's principles and can lead to healing and restoration.

5. Matthew 6:14-15 (ESV) "For if you forgive others their trespasses, your heavenly Father will also forgive you, but if you do not forgive others their trespasses, neither will your Father forgive your trespasses."

These verses emphasize the connection between our willingness to forgive others and receiving forgiveness from God. They underscore the importance of forgiving those who have hurt us as an integral part of our Christian walk.

6. Job 42:8-10 (ESV) "Now therefore take seven bulls and seven rams and go to my servant Job and offer up a burnt offering for yourselves. And my servant Job shall pray for you, for I will accept his prayer not to deal with you according to your folly. For you have not spoken of me what is right, as my servant Job has." So Eliphaz the Temanite and Bildad the Shuhite and Zophar the Naamathite went and did what the Lord had told them, and the Lord accepted Job's prayer."

Job's response to the hurt inflicted upon him by his friends demonstrates humility, forgiveness, and intercession. Despite their misguided words, Job interceded for them and demonstrated a heart of forgiveness.

7. Ephesians 4:31-32 (ESV) "Let all bitterness and wrath and anger and clamor and slander be put away from you, along with all malice. Be kind to one another, tenderhearted, forgiving one another, as God in Christ forgave you."

These verses highlight the importance of letting go of negative emotions and attitudes and replacing them with kindness, compassion, and forgiveness. We are called to forgive others as God has forgiven us.

8. Proverbs 14:30 (ASV) "A tranquil heart gives life to the flesh, but envy makes the bones rot."

This verse reminds us that holding onto hurt, anger, and bitterness can have detrimental effects on our well-being. Choosing forgiveness and seeking reconciliation promotes emotional and spiritual health.

9. Proverbs 11:17 (ESV) "A man who is kind benefits himself, but a cruel man hurts himself."

Responding to hurt with kindness and forgiveness benefits not only the other person but also ourselves. It frees us from the burden of anger and promotes positive relationships.

10. Romans 12:19-21 (ESV) "Beloved, never avenge yourselves, but leave it to the wrath of God, for it is written, 'Vengeance is mine, I will repay, says the Lord.' To the contrary, 'if your enemy is hungry, feed him; if he is thirsty, give him something to drink; for by so doing you will heap burning coals on his head.' Do not be overcome by evil, but overcome evil with good."

These verses teach us to leave judgment and vengeance to God and instead respond to hurt with acts of kindness and love. Responding in this way can potentially lead to conviction and change in the person who has hurt us.

How should we react to attacks from outside the church? (Luke 6:27-28; Matthew 5:10; 1 Peter 3:9; Romans 12:21; Ephesians 6:12)

How to React to Attacks from Outside the Church

When facing attacks or persecution from those outside the church, the Bible provides guidance on how believers should respond with love, grace, and a godly attitude. Let's explore the relevant scriptures:

1. Luke 6:27-28 (ESV): Love Your Enemies "But I say to you who hear, Love your enemies, do good to those who hate you, bless those who curse you, pray for those who abuse you."

Jesus teaches us to respond to attacks with love and kindness. Instead of retaliating, we are called to show love, extend acts of kindness, and pray for those who mistreat us.

2. Matthew 5:10 (ESV): Blessed Are the Persecuted "Blessed are those who are persecuted for righteousness' sake, for theirs is the kingdom of heaven."

Jesus assures believers that they are blessed when they face persecution for their faith. This perspective encourages us to endure and respond with faithfulness to God's calling, even in the face of opposition.

3. 1 Peter 3:9 (ESV) "Do not repay evil for evil or reviling for reviling, but on the contrary, bless, for to this you were called, that you may obtain a blessing."

Peter instructs believers not to repay evil with evil but to respond with blessings. Our calling is to bless others, even when faced with mistreatment or attacks, knowing that in doing so, we receive a blessing from God.

4. Romans 12:21 (ESV) "Do not be overcome by evil, but overcome evil with good."

Paul encourages believers to overcome evil with good. Rather than allowing attacks to fuel hatred or revenge, we are to respond with acts of kindness, forgiveness, and love, thus overcoming evil with the transforming power of good.

5. Ephesians 6:12 (ESV) "For we do not wrestle against flesh and blood, but against the rulers, against the authorities, against the cosmic powers over this present darkness, against the spiritual forces of evil in the heavenly places."

This verse reminds us that our ultimate battle is not against human opponents but against spiritual forces of evil. It encourages us to approach attacks from a spiritual perspective, relying on God's strength and spiritual armor to stand firm in faith.

To whom does God show mercy? (Matthew 6:14-15)

The Bible teaches us about God's mercy and reveals the recipients of His mercy. Let's explore the relevant scripture:

Matthew 6:14-15 (ESV): Forgiveness and Mercy "For if you forgive others their trespasses, your heavenly Father will also forgive you, but if you do not forgive others their trespasses, neither will your Father forgive your trespasses."

In these verses, Jesus emphasizes the importance of forgiveness and its connection to receiving God's mercy. Those who extend forgiveness to others will experience God's forgiveness and mercy themselves. However, those who withhold forgiveness from others will not receive forgiveness from God.

The message conveyed here is that God shows mercy to those who demonstrate a merciful and forgiving spirit towards others. It reflects the principle of reciprocity, where our actions and attitudes towards others have consequences for how we experience God's mercy.

This teaching aligns with the broader biblical theme of God's mercy being extended to those who humble themselves, seek forgiveness, and show mercy to others. Throughout the Bible, we see examples of individuals who received God's mercy when they repented, turned to Him, and sought forgiveness.

Ultimately, God's mercy is available to all who come to Him with contrite hearts, acknowledging their need for His forgiveness and extending forgiveness to others. His mercy knows no bounds and is extended to those who demonstrate a humble and merciful attitude towards their fellow human beings.

In summary, according to Matthew 6:14-15, God shows mercy to those who demonstrate a merciful and forgiving spirit towards others. By extending forgiveness to others, we open ourselves to receiving God's forgiveness and experiencing His abundant mercy.

Why is harboring resentment damaging? (Ephesians 4:31-32)

Resentment, or harboring bitterness and anger towards others, is a destructive emotion that can have serious consequences for our well-being and relationships. Let's explore the relevant scripture:

Ephesians 4:31-32 (ESV): Letting Go of Resentment "Let all bitterness and wrath and anger and clamor and slander be put away from you, along with all malice. Be kind to one another, tenderhearted, forgiving one another, as God in Christ forgave you."

In these verses, the apostle Paul addresses the damaging effects of harboring resentment. He urges believers to rid themselves of bitterness, anger, and malice, and instead cultivate kindness, tenderheartedness, and forgiveness.

Resentment not only affects our emotional well-being but also hinders our ability to maintain healthy relationships. It breeds a toxic environment characterized by bitterness, anger, and slander. It can lead to broken friendships, fractured families, and strained communities.

The passage encourages believers to let go of resentment and embrace forgiveness. By forgiving others, we free ourselves from the burden of carrying grudges and negative emotions. It allows us to experience healing and restoration in our relationships, both with others and with God.

Furthermore, the verse reminds us of God's example of forgiveness through Christ. As recipients of God's forgiveness, we are called to extend that same forgiveness to others. We are to imitate Christ's sacrificial love and mercy, seeking reconciliation rather than holding onto resentment.

From a psychological perspective, harboring resentment can negatively impact our mental and emotional well-being. It can lead to increased stress, anxiety, and even physical health problems. In contrast, practicing forgiveness and letting go of resentment promotes emotional healing, inner peace, and healthier relationships.

What does the Bible say about seeking revenge? (Romans 12:19-21)

Seeking revenge, or taking personal vengeance against those who have wronged us, is contrary to the teachings of the Bible. Let's explore the relevant scripture:

Romans 12:19-21 (ESV): Leaving Vengeance to God "Beloved, never avenge yourselves, but leave it to the wrath of God, for it is written, 'Vengeance is mine, I will repay, says the Lord.' To the contrary, 'if your enemy is hungry, feed him; if he is thirsty, give him something to drink; for by so doing you will heap burning coals on his head.' Do not be overcome by evil, but overcome evil with good."

In this passage, the apostle Paul addresses the concept of seeking revenge. He advises believers not to take matters into their own hands but to trust in God's justice and providence. Seeking revenge can lead to a cycle of violence and perpetuate a spirit of hostility, hindering forgiveness, reconciliation, and healing.

Instead, Paul encourages believers to respond to mistreatment with acts of kindness and love. By showing compassion and meeting the needs of our enemies, we exhibit Christ-like behavior. This approach not only confounds our adversaries but also demonstrates God's transformative power to overcome evil with good.

The passage emphasizes that leaving vengeance to God does not mean condoning or enabling wrongdoing. It recognizes that ultimate justice belongs to the Lord, who will repay according to His perfect wisdom and righteousness. Our role is to trust in God's sovereignty and follow the example of Christ, who forgave His enemies even as He suffered unjustly.

From a psychological standpoint, seeking revenge often leads to a cycle of anger, bitterness, and further harm. It can consume our thoughts, disrupt our emotional well-being, and hinder our ability to experience true forgiveness and inner peace. By entrusting justice to God and focusing on acts of kindness and love, we break free from the destructive cycle of revenge and allow God's healing power to work in our lives.

In summary, Romans 12:19-21 teaches that seeking revenge is contrary to God's will. Instead, believers are called to trust in God's justice, respond to mistreatment with acts of kindness, and overcome evil with good. By doing so, we demonstrate Christ-like behavior, promote reconciliation, and experience the transformative power of God's love in our lives. Seeking revenge only perpetuates harm, while leaving vengeance to God leads to healing and restoration.

Recognizing and Admitting Anger

The first step towards controlling anger is recognizing and admitting that it is a problem. In Psalm 38:18 (ESV), King David confesses, "I confess my iniquity; I am sorry for my sin." Acknowledging our anger honestly before God is the beginning of healing.

Understanding the Source of Anger

Anger often stems from unmet expectations, feelings of injustice, or personal hurts. It's crucial to identify the underlying cause of your anger and seek God's wisdom and guidance in addressing it. James 1:5 (ESV) encourages, "If any of you lacks wisdom, let him ask God, who gives generously to all without reproach, and it will be given him."

Biblical View of Anger

The Bible does not condemn anger per se; instead, it advises against sinning in our anger. Ephesians 4:26 (ESV) states, "Be angry and do not sin; do not let the sun go down on your anger." It's essential to differentiate between righteous anger, which is a response to sin and injustice, and unrighteous anger, which is often rooted in selfishness and pride.

Using God's Word to Counteract Anger

God's Word is an effective tool for counteracting anger. Meditating on God's promises, like those found in Psalm 37:8 (ASV), can help defuse anger: "Cease from anger, and forsake wrath: fret not thyself, it tendeth only to evil doing."

Developing New Responses

Part of managing anger involves learning new, healthier responses. This can be achieved through a combination of biblical principles and practical techniques. For example, practicing patience, a virtue praised in Proverbs 14:29 (ASV), "He that is slow to anger is of great understanding," and using Cognitive Behavioral Therapy methods to reframe negative thinking patterns can be beneficial.

The Role of Forgiveness

Forgiveness is a powerful antidote to anger. It does not justify the wrong, but it releases the burden of resentment. In Ephesians 4:32 (ESV), we are instructed, "Be kind to one another, tenderhearted, forgiving one another, as God in Christ forgave you."

Prayer and Dependence on God

We should consistently seek God's help in controlling our anger. Psalm 141:3 (ASV) presents a great prayer for this: "Set a watch, O Jehovah, before my mouth; Keep the door of my lips."

Involvement of Community

Christian community can offer support, accountability, and encouragement in our journey towards managing anger. James 5:16 (ESV) says, "Therefore, confess your sins to one another and pray for one another, that you may be healed."

Relying on the Holy Spirit

The Holy Spirit empowers us to exhibit self-control, one of the fruits of the Spirit as outlined in Galatians 5:22-23 (ESV), which is essential for managing anger.

The Anger Spectrum: Frustration, Annoyance, and Wrath

Anger exists on a spectrum, ranging from minor annoyance to full-blown wrath. Understanding where our anger falls on this spectrum can help us address it appropriately. Paul writes in Romans 12:19 (ESV), "Beloved, never avenge yourselves, but leave it to the wrath of God, for it is written, 'Vengeance is mine, I will repay, says the Lord.'"

Understanding and Expressing Anger Appropriately

Anger is a natural emotion, but it can become destructive when not expressed appropriately. Learning to express anger in a healthy way - articulating feelings without aggression, taking a time-out when emotions rise - can make a significant difference in our relationships and overall well-being. "A soft answer turns away wrath, but a harsh word stirs up anger," we read in Proverbs 15:1 (ESV).

Applying the Golden Rule

The 'Golden Rule' is a Biblical principle that can guide us in our responses to anger-inducing situations. In Matthew 7:12 (ESV), Jesus advises, "So whatever you wish that others would do to you, do also to them, for this is the Law and the Prophets." Before reacting in anger, we should consider if we would appreciate being on the receiving end of our planned response.

Letting Go of Control

Often, our anger stems from situations beyond our control. Recognizing that we can't control others' actions but only our reactions can alleviate anger. In Proverbs 19:21 (ASV), we learn, "There are many devices in a man's heart; But the counsel of Jehovah, that shall stand."

Training in Emotional Intelligence

Learning to recognize, understand, and manage our emotions - Emotional Intelligence - can be valuable in controlling anger. It involves empathy, self-awareness, and effective communication. Jesus modeled these qualities throughout his earthly ministry.

The Transforming Power of God's Love

The love of God has a transformative power that can alter our perspectives and responses. As we experience and understand God's unconditional love, our hearts soften, and we can more easily let go of anger. 1 John 4:19 (ESV) reminds us, "We love because he first loved us."

Transforming Anger into Positive Action

Righteous anger can be used positively to spur us into action against injustice. This is clear in the example of Jesus in the temple (John 2:13-17 ESV), where His anger against the desecration of His Father's house led Him to act.

Finding Peace Amidst Anger

Ultimately, controlling anger is about finding peace - peace with God, peace with others, and peace within ourselves. Jesus offers this peace to us. In John 14:27 (ESV), He says, "Peace I leave with you; my peace I give to you. Not as the world gives do I give to you. Let not your hearts be troubled, neither let them be afraid."

In gaining control over anger, it is crucial to understand that it is a gradual process requiring continuous effort, commitment, and reliance on God. By implementing these biblical principles and practical strategies, we can experience victory over anger, leading to a more peaceful and fulfilling life.

Recognize Triggers and Symptoms

The first step is understanding what provokes your anger and how it manifests physically and emotionally. Triggers could include certain people, conversations, or situations. Symptoms might include a racing heart, tense muscles, or feeling hot. Once you identify these, you can be better prepared to handle anger when it arises.

Question Irrational Thoughts

CBT emphasizes the role of cognitive distortions or irrational thoughts in creating and exacerbating emotional responses like anger. When you notice yourself becoming angry, ask yourself what thoughts are going through your mind. Then challenge these thoughts. Are they realistic? Are they helpful? Would you think the same way if you were calm? The Apostle Paul exhorts us in 2 Corinthians 10:5 (ESV) to "take every thought captive to obey Christ."

Reframe Thoughts

Once you've identified and questioned irrational thoughts, the next step is reframing them. This is a technique called cognitive restructuring. Instead of thinking, "This is unbearable, I can't stand this," you might reframe that to, "This is frustrating, but getting angry won't resolve anything."

Practice Mindfulness

Mindfulness, being fully present in the moment, can help manage anger. When anger arises, try to step back and observe your feelings without judgment. Rather than reacting impulsively, choose a thoughtful response. In Proverbs 29:11 (ESV), we read, "A fool gives full vent to his spirit, but a wise man quietly holds it back."

Use Relaxation Techniques

Relaxation techniques such as deep breathing, progressive muscle relaxation, or visualization can help dissipate anger. These methods reduce the physiological arousal that anger causes and promote calmness. "Be still, and know that I am God," Psalm 46:10 (ASV) reminds us.

Assertive Communication

Expressing your feelings and needs assertively rather than aggressively can help manage anger. Assertive communication respects your rights and the rights of others, reducing the chance of conflict. Ephesians 4:15 (ESV) encourages us to speak "the truth in love."

Problem-Solving

If your anger is caused by a problem or situation that can be changed, work on finding a solution. This proactive approach can prevent feelings of helplessness and frustration that might lead to anger. In Philippians 4:13 (ESV), Paul writes, "I can do all things through him who strengthens me."

Practicing Forgiveness

Holding onto anger often leads to resentment and bitterness. Practicing forgiveness, as God forgives us (Ephesians 4:32, ESV), can release you from the burden of anger and lead to peace.

In conclusion, controlling anger involves a multi-faceted approach that combines Biblical teachings, Cognitive Behavioral Therapy techniques, and practical strategies. Remember, overcoming anger is a journey and there will be challenges along the way. But with perseverance and God's guidance, you can successfully manage and control your anger.

CHAPTER 9 How Do You Get Control Over Obsessive Control Behaviors?

Questions and Answers

What causes Obsessive Control Disorder? How can it be relieved?

Obsessive Control Disorder, often referred to as Obsessive-Compulsive Disorder (OCD), is a mental health condition characterized by recurring, intrusive thoughts (obsessions) and repetitive behaviors (compulsions) that individuals feel driven to perform. While the exact cause of OCD is not fully understood, it is likely influenced by a combination of biological, genetic, and environmental factors. The Bible provides wisdom and guidance that can be helpful in managing and finding relief from OCD symptoms.

Understanding OCD through Scripture

1. **Psalm 139:14 (ASV): Recognizing Our Value** "I will give thanks unto thee; for I am fearfully and wonderfully made: Wonderful are thy works; And that my soul knoweth right well."

This verse reminds us of our intrinsic worth and value as creations of God. Understanding that we are fearfully and wonderfully made can counteract feelings of inadequacy or the need to control every aspect of life. Embracing our identity as cherished individuals can help alleviate obsessive thoughts and the need for excessive control.

2. **Philippians 4:6-7 (ESV): Finding Peace in God** "Do not be anxious about anything, but in everything by prayer and supplication with thanksgiving let your requests be made known to God. And the peace of God, which surpasses all

understanding, will guard your hearts and your minds in Christ Jesus."

This passage encourages believers to bring their concerns and anxieties to God through prayer. By surrendering control to Him and seeking His guidance and peace, individuals with OCD can find relief from obsessive thoughts and compulsive behaviors. Trusting in God's sovereignty and seeking His comfort can alleviate the need to excessively control every aspect of life.

Relieving Obsessive Control Disorder

1. **Seek Professional Help** Consulting with a mental health professional, such as a psychologist or psychiatrist, is essential in managing and treating OCD. These professionals can provide a comprehensive assessment, develop a tailored treatment plan, and guide individuals through evidence-based therapies like Cognitive-Behavioral Therapy (CBT) or medication, if necessary.

2. **Practice Mindfulness and Acceptance** Mindfulness techniques, such as deep breathing exercises and meditation, can help individuals with OCD redirect their focus away from obsessive thoughts and reduce anxiety. Acceptance-based approaches, like Acceptance and Commitment Therapy (ACT), can assist in recognizing and accepting unwanted thoughts without acting on compulsions, fostering a healthier relationship with uncertainty.

3. **Build a Supportive Community** Surrounding oneself with understanding and supportive individuals, such as family, friends, or support groups, can provide encouragement and empathy. Sharing experiences and finding solace in a community can help individuals with OCD feel understood and lessen the burden of excessive control.

4. **Apply Scriptural Wisdom** Applying biblical principles, such as surrendering control to God, seeking His peace through prayer, and recognizing our inherent worth, can bring spiritual and emotional relief. By aligning thoughts and actions with

God's Word, individuals can find comfort and reassurance, allowing them to manage OCD symptoms more effectively.

It is important to remember that seeking professional help and integrating biblical principles into daily life can work hand in hand to provide comprehensive support and relief for individuals with Obsessive Control Disorder.

But what if obsessive thoughts seem irreverent or blasphemous?

Obsessive thoughts that seem irreverent or blasphemous can be distressing and cause significant anxiety for individuals. It is important to recognize that these thoughts are often a manifestation of Obsessive-Compulsive Disorder (OCD) and do not reflect one's true beliefs or intentions. The Bible provides guidance and reassurance for those struggling with such thoughts.

Understanding Obsessive Thoughts through Scripture

1. **2 Corinthians 10:5 (ESV): Taking Every Thought Captive**
   "We destroy arguments and every lofty opinion raised against the knowledge of God, and take every thought captive to obey Christ."

This verse reminds believers of the importance of taking control of their thoughts and aligning them with the truth of God's Word. For those experiencing intrusive or disturbing thoughts, the act of "taking every thought captive" involves recognizing that these thoughts do not define one's character or relationship with God.

2. **Philippians 4:8 (ASV): Focusing on the Right Things**
   "Finally, brethren, whatsoever things are true, whatsoever things are honorable, whatsoever things are just, whatsoever things are pure, whatsoever things are lovely, whatsoever things are of good report; if there be any virtue, and if there be any praise, think on these things."

This passage encourages believers to focus their minds on thoughts that are true, honorable, just, pure, lovely, and praiseworthy.

By redirecting attention to positive and uplifting thoughts, individuals can counteract intrusive or disturbing thoughts, including those that may seem irreverent or blasphemous.

Finding Relief and Seeking Help

1. **Understand the Nature of OCD** Recognize that OCD is a mental health condition characterized by intrusive and unwanted thoughts. These thoughts often go against one's true beliefs and values. Understanding the nature of OCD can help individuals separate their true identity and intentions from the intrusive thoughts they experience.

2. **Seek Professional Guidance** Consult with a mental health professional who specializes in OCD or anxiety disorders. They can provide a proper diagnosis and develop a treatment plan tailored to the individual's needs. Cognitive-Behavioral Therapy (CBT), including Exposure and Response Prevention (ERP), is a highly effective treatment approach for managing OCD symptoms.

3. **Practice Acceptance and Mindfulness** Embrace acceptance-based approaches, such as Acceptance and Commitment Therapy (ACT) or mindfulness techniques, to help manage distressing thoughts. By acknowledging and accepting the presence of these thoughts without judgment, individuals can reduce the anxiety they cause and gain a greater sense of control over their reactions.

4. **Utilize Supportive Resources** Engage in support groups or seek support from a community of individuals who understand OCD and its associated challenges. Sharing experiences, receiving encouragement, and learning from others' strategies can provide valuable insights and emotional support.

5. **Continue Spiritual Nourishment** Maintain a close relationship with God through prayer, reading His Word, and seeking His guidance. Remember that God understands our hearts and intentions. Confessing intrusive thoughts and seeking His forgiveness can bring peace and assurance.

It is important to seek professional help and utilize both psychological and spiritual resources to manage and find relief from OCD symptoms. Remember that having intrusive thoughts does not reflect one's true character or beliefs, and with proper support and strategies, individuals can find healing and restoration.

What feelings or thoughts typically precede compulsive behavior?

When it comes to compulsive behavior, there are certain feelings and thoughts that often precede the urge to engage in repetitive actions or rituals. These thoughts and emotions can vary from person to person and depend on the specific nature of their compulsions. While the Bible does not explicitly address the concept of compulsive behavior, it provides guidance on managing our thoughts and emotions.

Understanding the Patterns of Compulsive Behavior

1. **Anxiety and Fear** Many individuals experience heightened anxiety and fear before engaging in compulsive behaviors. These emotions can arise from a variety of triggers, such as obsessive thoughts, the fear of something going wrong, or the need for control and certainty.

2. **Obsessive Thoughts** Obsessive thoughts are often intrusive and repetitive, causing distress and leading to compulsive behaviors as an attempt to alleviate anxiety. These thoughts can be persistent and difficult to ignore, resulting in the urge to engage in specific rituals or repetitive actions.

3. **Sense of Urgency** Individuals may feel a strong sense of urgency or pressure to perform certain behaviors or rituals to prevent a perceived negative outcome or to maintain a sense of safety and control.

4. **Temporary Relief or Gratification** Compulsive behaviors can provide temporary relief or a sense of gratification. The immediate reduction in anxiety or distress reinforces the

connection between the behavior and the relief, further reinforcing the cycle of compulsive behavior.

Biblical Principles for Managing Thoughts and Emotions

1. **2 Corinthians 10:5 (ESV): Taking Thoughts Captive** "We destroy arguments and every lofty opinion raised against the knowledge of God, and take every thought captive to obey Christ."

This verse encourages believers to take control of their thoughts and align them with the truth of God's Word. By recognizing and challenging negative or intrusive thoughts, individuals can interrupt the cycle of compulsive behavior.

2. **Philippians 4:6-7 (ASV): Casting Anxiety on God** "In nothing be anxious; but in everything by prayer and supplication with thanksgiving let your requests be made known unto God. And the peace of God, which passeth all understanding, shall guard your hearts and your thoughts in Christ Jesus."

These verses remind believers to bring their anxieties and concerns to God through prayer, trusting Him to provide peace and comfort. By surrendering our worries to God, we can find solace and reduce the intensity of anxiety that often drives compulsive behavior.

3. **Romans 12:2 (ESV): Renewing the Mind** "Do not be conformed to this world, but be transformed by the renewal of your mind, that by testing you may discern what is the will of God, what is good and acceptable and perfect."

Renewing the mind through the Word of God is crucial for managing thoughts and emotions. By immersing ourselves in Scripture, we gain wisdom, discernment, and the ability to challenge unhelpful thought patterns.

4. **James 4:7-8 (ESV): Submitting to God and Resisting the Devil** "Submit yourselves therefore to God. Resist the devil, and he will flee from you. Draw near to God, and he will draw near to you."

Submitting to God and resisting the temptations of the enemy can help individuals break free from the cycles of compulsive behavior. Drawing near to God through prayer, worship, and seeking His guidance allows us to find strength and overcome the patterns that contribute to our compulsions.

While the Bible does not explicitly address the topic of compulsive behavior, it offers timeless principles for managing our thoughts and emotions. Combining these principles with professional help and evidence-based treatments can provide individuals with a holistic approach to finding relief and healing from compulsive behaviors.

How does one usually feel during compulsive behavior?

Feelings During Compulsive Behavior

When individuals engage in compulsive behavior, they often experience a range of emotions and feelings. While the Bible does not specifically address compulsive behavior, it provides insights into human nature and emotions that can help us understand the experiences of those struggling with compulsions.

1. Anxiety and Fear Compulsive behavior is often driven by anxiety and fear. Individuals may feel a heightened sense of worry, apprehension, or unease. They may fear that something bad will happen if they don't engage in their compulsive behaviors or rituals. These feelings of anxiety can be intense and overwhelming.

2. Urgency and Tension During compulsive behavior, individuals often feel a sense of urgency and tension. They may experience a strong internal pressure to perform certain actions or rituals immediately. This urgency can be difficult to resist and may increase the intensity of the compulsive behavior.

3. Relief or Temporary Satisfaction Engaging in compulsive behavior can provide temporary relief or a sense of satisfaction. Individuals may experience a momentary reduction in anxiety or discomfort after performing their rituals. This relief reinforces the connection between the behavior and the temporary alleviation of distress, further reinforcing the compulsion.

4. Frustration and Guilt While compulsive behavior may temporarily relieve anxiety, individuals often experience frustration and guilt afterward. They may feel frustrated with themselves for being unable to resist the compulsions or guilty for spending excessive time and energy on repetitive behaviors.

Biblical Insights on Emotions and Coping

Although the Bible does not specifically address compulsive behavior, it provides guidance on managing emotions and finding strength in challenging situations.

1. Philippians 4:6-7 (ESV): Trusting in God's Peace "Do not be anxious about anything, but in everything by prayer and supplication with thanksgiving let your requests be made known to God. And the peace of God, which surpasses all understanding, will guard your hearts and your minds in Christ Jesus."

This passage encourages individuals to bring their anxieties and concerns to God through prayer. By trusting in God's peace, we can find solace and a sense of calm even in the midst of our struggles.

2. Psalm 34:17-18 (ASV): Seeking God's Help "The righteous cry out, and Jehovah hears them; he delivers them from all their troubles. Jehovah is close to the brokenhearted and saves those who are crushed in spirit."

When facing the challenges of compulsive behavior, we can turn to God for help and deliverance. He is near to those who are hurting and offers comfort and support in times of distress.

3. Psalm 46:1 (ESV): Finding Strength in God "God is our refuge and strength, a very present help in trouble."

God is our source of strength and refuge. When we feel overwhelmed by compulsive behavior, we can find comfort and strength in knowing that He is with us and will provide the help we need.

4. 2 Corinthians 12:9 (ESV): God's Grace in Weakness "But he said to me, 'My grace is sufficient for you, for my power is made perfect in weakness.' Therefore I will boast all the more gladly of my weaknesses, so that the power of Christ may rest upon me."

Even in our struggles with compulsive behavior, God's grace is sufficient. He can work through our weaknesses and provide the strength we need to resist and overcome the grip of compulsion.

While the Bible does not provide specific guidance on compulsive behavior, its teachings on trust, seeking God's help, finding strength in Him, and relying on His grace can offer comfort and encouragement to those struggling with compulsions. Additionally, seeking professional help, such as therapy or counseling, can be beneficial in understanding and addressing the underlying causes of compulsive behavior.

What consequences or feelings arise after engaging in compulsive behavior?

Engaging in compulsive behavior can have various consequences and evoke specific feelings and emotions. While the Bible does not specifically address compulsive behavior, it provides insights into human nature, consequences of actions, and the importance of finding strength and forgiveness through God's grace.

1. Temporary Relief Followed by Disappointment After engaging in compulsive behavior, individuals may experience temporary relief or a sense of satisfaction. However, this relief is often short-lived, and disappointment or dissatisfaction may quickly follow. The compulsive behavior may not provide the expected long-term solution to underlying anxieties or distress.

2. Increased Guilt and Shame Compulsive behaviors can lead to feelings of guilt and shame. Individuals may be aware that their behaviors are excessive or irrational, which can contribute to negative self-perception and a sense of moral wrongdoing. These feelings can create a cycle of guilt and shame that perpetuates the compulsive behavior.

3. Frustration and Loss of Control Repeated engagement in compulsive behavior can lead to frustration and a sense of loss of control. Individuals may feel trapped in a pattern they cannot break, despite their desire to stop or reduce the behaviors. This loss of control can intensify feelings of frustration and hopelessness.

4. Interference with Daily Life and Relationships Compulsive behaviors can interfere with various aspects of life, including relationships, work or school performance, and overall functioning. This interference can lead to strained relationships, isolation, and a reduced quality of life. It may be challenging to maintain healthy relationships and fulfill responsibilities due to the time and energy consumed by compulsive behaviors.

Biblical Insights on Consequences and Redemption

While the Bible does not directly address the consequences of compulsive behavior, it offers guidance on the nature of sin, the consequences of our actions, and the hope of redemption through God's grace.

1. Romans 6:23 (ESV): Consequences of Sin "For the wages of sin is death, but the free gift of God is eternal life in Christ Jesus our Lord."

Sin, including compulsive behavior, has consequences. It can lead to spiritual and emotional death, as well as negative effects on our well-being and relationships. Recognizing the negative consequences of our actions can motivate us to seek change and healing.

2. Psalm 103:8-12 (ASV): God's Forgiveness and Redemption "The LORD is merciful and gracious, slow to anger and abounding in steadfast love. He will not always chide, nor will he keep his anger forever. He does not deal with us according to our sins, nor repay us according to our iniquities. For as high as the heavens are above the earth, so great is his steadfast love toward those who fear him; as far as the east is from the west, so far does he remove our transgressions from us."

God's forgiveness and redemption are available to those who turn to Him in repentance. He is merciful, gracious, and loving, offering forgiveness and restoration to those who seek His forgiveness and strive to change their ways.

3. 1 John 1:9 (ESV): God's Faithfulness to Forgive "If we confess our sins, he is faithful and just to forgive us our sins and to cleanse us from all unrighteousness."

Confession and repentance are essential for finding forgiveness and healing. By acknowledging our sins and seeking God's forgiveness, we can experience His faithfulness in forgiving us and cleansing us from unrighteousness.

4. Isaiah 43:25 (ESV): God's Willingness to Remember Sin No More "I, I am he who blots out your transgressions for my own sake, and I will not remember your sins."

When we seek God's forgiveness, He not only forgives but also chooses not to remember our sins. Through His grace, He offers a fresh start and the opportunity to break free from the cycles of compulsive behavior.

While these verses do not specifically address compulsive behavior, they provide a foundation for understanding God's willingness to forgive, cleanse, and restore. Through faith, repentance, and reliance on God's grace, individuals can find hope, healing, and strength to overcome compulsive behaviors and cultivate a healthier life.

It's important to note that seeking professional help from Christian mental health professionals, such as therapists or counselors, can also be beneficial in addressing and managing compulsive behaviors.

What are the situations or environments that often trigger compulsive behavior?

Situation and Environments that Often Trigger Compulsive Behavior

Compulsive behavior can be triggered by various situations or environments. While the Bible does not explicitly address compulsive behavior triggers, it provides wisdom and guidance on self-control, avoiding temptation, and seeking God's help in overcoming challenges.

1. Proverbs 4:14-15 (ASV): Avoiding the Path of the Wicked "Enter not into the path of the wicked, and walk not in the way of evil men. Avoid it, pass not by it; turn from it, and pass on."

Avoiding environments or situations associated with sinful behaviors can help prevent the triggering of compulsive behavior. The Bible encourages us to stay away from the paths of the wicked and to choose a righteous path instead.

2. Matthew 26:41 (ESV): Vigilance and Prayer "Watch and pray that you may not enter into temptation. The spirit indeed is willing, but the flesh is weak."

Vigilance and prayer are essential in resisting temptations and avoiding situations that may trigger compulsive behavior. By staying alert and seeking God's guidance, we can find strength to overcome the challenges we face.

3. Psalm 119:11 (ESV): Storing God's Word in the Heart "I have stored up your word in my heart, that I might not sin against you."

Knowing and internalizing God's Word can serve as a source of strength and guidance when facing triggers for compulsive behavior. By filling our hearts and minds with God's truth, we can resist temptations and make wise choices.

4. 1 Corinthians 10:13 (ESV): God's Faithfulness in Temptation "No temptation has overtaken you that is not common to man. God is faithful, and he will not let you be tempted beyond your ability, but with the temptation, he will also provide the way of escape, that you may be able to endure it."

God promises to provide a way of escape when we face temptations. Although specific triggers may vary among individuals,

God's faithfulness and grace are available to help us navigate through challenging situations.

5. James 4:7-8 (ESV): Submitting to God and Resisting the Devil "Submit yourselves therefore to God. Resist the devil, and he will flee from you. Draw near to God, and he will draw near to you."

By submitting to God, seeking His presence, and resisting the influence of the enemy, we can find strength to overcome compulsive behaviors triggered by worldly influences.

While the Bible does not provide an exhaustive list of specific triggers for compulsive behavior, it offers principles and guidance on making wise choices, resisting temptation, and relying on God's strength to overcome challenges. It emphasizes the importance of avoiding sinful environments, cultivating self-control, and seeking God's help in times of temptation. Additionally, seeking support from mental health professionals and engaging in therapy can be beneficial for identifying and managing specific triggers related to compulsive behaviors.

What are innocent appearing situations that can lead to compulsive behavior?

Compulsive behavior can be triggered by situations that may initially appear innocent or harmless. While the Bible does not specifically address innocent-appearing situations that lead to compulsive behavior, it provides principles and wisdom to help guide our actions and choices. By applying biblical principles, we can discern and avoid situations that may potentially lead to compulsive behavior.

1. Proverbs 7:6-23 (ASV): The Seductive Temptation This passage describes the encounter of a young man with a seductive woman. The situation initially appears innocent as she entices him with flattery and allure. However, the outcome is detrimental, leading to sin and its consequences. It serves as a cautionary tale to be vigilant and avoid situations that may lead to immoral behavior.

2. James 1:14-15 (ESV): The Progression of Temptation "But each person is tempted when he is lured and enticed by his own desire. Then desire, when it has conceived, gives birth to sin, and sin, when it is fully grown, brings forth death."

This passage highlights the progression of temptation, starting from the allure of desire. Innocent-seeming situations can slowly and subtly lead to compulsive behavior if not recognized and resisted. It emphasizes the importance of self-awareness and self-control in navigating these situations.

3. 1 Corinthians 10:12 (ESV): Guarding Against Overconfidence "Therefore let anyone who thinks that he stands take heed lest he fall."

Even in seemingly innocent situations, it is crucial to exercise caution and humility. Overconfidence can lead to vulnerability and give way to compulsive behaviors. Recognizing our susceptibility to temptation reminds us of the need for vigilance and reliance on God's strength.

4. Proverbs 4:23 (ASV): Guarding the Heart "Above all else, guard your heart, for everything you do flows from it."

This verse highlights the importance of guarding our hearts and minds. Innocent-seeming situations can impact our thoughts, emotions, and behaviors. By cultivating a heart that is aligned with God's truth and wisdom, we can discern and navigate through potentially harmful situations.

While the Bible does not provide an exhaustive list of innocent-appearing situations that can lead to compulsive behavior, it offers principles and guidance to help us make wise choices. It encourages us to be vigilant, guard our hearts, and rely on God's wisdom and strength to navigate through various temptations and challenges we may encounter. Additionally, seeking guidance from trusted mentors, counselors, or mental health professionals can provide additional support in identifying and addressing specific triggers related to compulsive behavior.

How does the behavior usually impact one's life – socially, professionally, personally, or health-wise?

Impact of Compulsive Behavior on Various Areas of Life

Compulsive behavior can have far-reaching consequences that affect different aspects of a person's life. While the Bible does not specifically address the impact of compulsive behavior, it provides wisdom and principles that can be applied to understand the potential consequences. Here are some general insights on how compulsive behavior can impact one's life:

1. Social Impact Compulsive behavior can significantly impact a person's social life. It may lead to strained relationships, isolation, and withdrawal from social activities. Compulsive behaviors can consume a person's time and attention, making it difficult to engage in healthy social interactions and maintain meaningful connections with others.

2. Professional Impact Compulsive behavior can also affect one's professional life. It may lead to decreased productivity, poor performance, and difficulties in meeting responsibilities and commitments. Additionally, the preoccupation with compulsive behaviors can interfere with career advancement opportunities and negatively impact professional relationships.

3. Personal Impact On a personal level, compulsive behavior can cause emotional distress, guilt, and a loss of self-control. It can erode self-esteem, leading to feelings of shame and inadequacy. Additionally, compulsive behaviors can disrupt personal goals and aspirations, hindering personal growth and fulfillment.

4. Health Impact Compulsive behavior can have adverse effects on physical and mental health. The stress and anxiety associated with compulsive behaviors can contribute to various health issues, including insomnia, high blood pressure, digestive problems, and compromised immune function. Furthermore, engaging in harmful or risky behaviors as a result of compulsions can jeopardize one's overall well-being.

While the Bible does not provide specific guidance on the consequences of compulsive behavior, it does emphasize the importance of self-control, moderation, and seeking God's wisdom in all aspects of life. Proverbs 25:28 (ESV) states, "A man without self-control is like a city broken into and left without walls." This verse underscores the significance of exercising self-control to safeguard one's life and well-being.

It is important for individuals struggling with compulsive behavior to seek appropriate support and professional help. Through therapy, counseling, and support groups, individuals can develop strategies to manage their compulsions and work towards healthier patterns of behavior. By integrating biblical principles with professional guidance, individuals can address the impact of compulsive behavior on their lives and strive for positive change.

What strategies have can one try to control or stop this behavior?

Strategies for Controlling or Stopping Compulsive Behavior

Overcoming compulsive behavior requires a comprehensive approach that combines biblical principles, professional guidance, and personal effort. While the Bible does not provide specific strategies for addressing compulsive behavior, it offers wisdom and guidance that can be applied to promote self-control and healthy habits. Here are some general strategies to consider:

1. Seek God's Guidance and Strength Turn to God in prayer, seeking His guidance and strength to overcome compulsive behavior. Philippians 4:13 (ESV) declares, "I can do all things through him who strengthens me." Relying on God's power can provide the necessary strength to resist compulsions and pursue healthier choices.

2. Renew Your Mind Transform your thinking by aligning your thoughts with God's truth. Romans 12:2 (ESV) instructs, "Do not be conformed to this world, but be transformed by the renewal of your mind." Replace negative thought patterns and beliefs that contribute to compulsive behavior with God's Word and promises. Fill your mind with thoughts that promote self-control, discipline, and godly virtues.

3. Develop a Support System Surround yourself with a supportive community of like-minded individuals who can encourage, pray for, and hold you accountable in your journey to overcome compulsive behavior. Ecclesiastes 4:9-10 (ESV) emphasizes the strength found in community, stating, "Two are better than one, because they have a good reward for their toil. For if they fall, one will lift up his fellow."

4. Practice Self-Reflection and Awareness Engage in self-reflection to identify triggers, patterns, and underlying emotions associated with compulsive behavior. Proverbs 14:8 (ESV) advises, "The wisdom of the prudent is to discern his way." By understanding the root causes of compulsions, you can develop strategies to address them effectively.

5. Seek Professional Help Consider seeking professional help from therapists, counselors, or support groups specializing in behavioral and addiction issues. They can provide valuable tools, strategies, and techniques to help you gain control over compulsive behavior.

6. Replace Harmful Behaviors with Positive Alternatives Instead of engaging in compulsive behavior, redirect your energy towards healthy and productive activities. Fill your time with activities that align with your values and contribute to personal growth, such as pursuing hobbies, engaging in physical exercise, volunteering, or developing new skills.

7. Practice Self-Care Prioritize self-care to maintain overall well-being. Take care of your physical, emotional, and spiritual needs. This includes adequate rest, nourishing your body with healthy foods, engaging in regular exercise, and nurturing your relationship with God through prayer, meditation, and study of His Word.

While these strategies are not specific to compulsive behavior, they align with biblical principles of self-control, renewal of the mind, seeking God's guidance, and embracing community. By combining these strategies with professional guidance, individuals can take significant steps towards controlling or stopping compulsive behavior and pursuing a healthier, more balanced life.

What support systems does one need to have in place?

Support Systems for Overcoming Compulsive Behavior

When dealing with compulsive behavior, having a strong support system in place is crucial for encouragement, accountability, and guidance. While the Bible does not provide specific instructions on support systems for overcoming compulsive behavior, it does emphasize the importance of community, fellowship, and seeking wise counsel. Here are some key support systems to consider:

1. Church Community Engage with a local church community where you can find spiritual guidance, encouragement, and fellowship. Hebrews 10:25 (ASV) encourages believers to gather together, stating, "Not forsaking our own assembling together, as the custom of some is, but exhorting one another; and so much the more, as ye see the day drawing nigh." Participating in a church community can provide you with a network of individuals who can offer support, prayer, and spiritual guidance.

2. Accountability Partners Seek out trustworthy individuals who can serve as accountability partners in your journey to overcome compulsive behavior. Proverbs 27:17 (ESV) states, "Iron sharpens iron, and one man sharpens another." Accountability partners can offer guidance, provide a listening ear, and hold you responsible for your actions. Choose someone who shares your faith and is committed to helping you grow and overcome your struggles.

3. Support Groups Consider joining support groups specifically tailored to address compulsive behavior or addiction. These groups provide a safe space to share experiences, gain insights, and receive support from others facing similar challenges. Galatians 6:2 (ESV) emphasizes bearing one another's burdens, stating, "Bear one another's burdens, and so fulfill the law of Christ." In a support group, you can find encouragement, empathy, and practical advice to help you navigate your journey toward freedom.

4. Professional Counselors and Therapists Seek professional help by engaging with qualified counselors or therapists who specialize in behavioral issues and addiction. They can provide personalized guidance, therapeutic interventions, and strategies to address the underlying causes of compulsive behavior. Proverbs 11:14 (ESV) highlights the value of seeking counsel, stating, "Where there is no guidance, a people falls, but in an abundance of counselors, there is safety."

5. Family and Friends Reach out to your close family members and friends who can offer emotional support, understanding, and encouragement. Proverbs 17:17 (ESV) emphasizes the significance of a loyal friend, stating, "A friend loves at all times, and a brother is born for adversity." Share your struggles with trusted loved ones who can provide a listening ear, offer prayer, and stand by your side as you work towards overcoming compulsive behavior.

6. Online Communities Explore online communities and forums dedicated to supporting individuals facing compulsive behavior. These communities can provide a platform for sharing experiences, seeking advice, and connecting with others who are on a similar journey of healing and restoration. While online support should not replace real-life relationships, it can be a valuable supplement to your support network.

Remember that each person's support system may look different based on their specific needs and circumstances. It is essential to surround yourself with individuals who genuinely care for your well-being, share your values, and are committed to helping you overcome compulsive behavior. Together with the support of your community, professional guidance, and personal determination, you can find the strength to break free from the grip of compulsive behavior.

Christian Counseling, Biblical Counseling, and Biblical Principles

Overcoming obsessive control behaviors requires a transformation not only of our actions but, more fundamentally, of our hearts. As we see in Jeremiah 17:9 (ASV), "The heart is deceitful above all things, and it is exceedingly corrupt: who can know it?" Our hearts dictate our actions, which means that change must begin at the deepest level of our being.

Finding Comfort in God's Sovereignty

A desire for control often stems from fear, insecurity, and a lack of trust in God's sovereignty. When we truly comprehend that God "works all things after the counsel of his will" (Ephesians 1:11, ESV), we can begin to release our compulsive need to control. God is the ultimate controller, and we can trust in His goodness and wisdom.

Practicing Submission and Humility

Learning to submit to God and others counters the self-centeredness often inherent in control behaviors. Submission and humility do not mean being a doormat; instead, they involve recognizing and respecting the rightful authority of others, including God. "Submit yourselves therefore to God" (James 4:7, ESV). Remember, "God opposes the proud, but gives grace to the humble" (James 4:6, ESV).

Developing Patience and Trust

Growing in patience involves trusting God's timing. When we try to control things, we are essentially saying that our timing is better than God's. But as we read in Ecclesiastes 3:1 (ASV), "For everything there is a season, and a time for every purpose under heaven."

Reaching Out for Support

Don't isolate yourself. Share your struggles with other believers. They can provide encouragement, accountability, and practical wisdom. As Galatians 6:2 (ESV) instructs, "Bear one another's burdens, and so fulfill the law of Christ."

Cognitive Behavioral Therapy (CBT) Tools and Practical Tips

Identify Triggers

Identify situations, thoughts, or feelings that trigger your obsessive control behaviors. By knowing your triggers, you can anticipate and better manage your responses.

Challenge Irrational Thoughts

Control behaviors often stem from irrational beliefs like "I must have control to be safe." Challenge these thoughts by asking, "Is this thought rational? What evidence supports or contradicts it? How likely is the scenario I fear?"

Cognitive Restructuring

Learn to replace irrational thoughts with rational ones. Instead of "I must control everything," consider, "While I prefer control, I can cope even when I don't have it."

Exposure Therapy

Gradually expose yourself to situations where you don't have control, starting with less anxiety-provoking circumstances and moving on to more challenging ones. This therapy can help you reduce your fear and discomfort over time.

Mindfulness and Relaxation Techniques

Practicing mindfulness and relaxation techniques can help reduce anxiety associated with lack of control. Mindfulness involves staying present and accepting the current situation without trying to change it.

Build Healthy Relationships

Obsessive control behaviors can strain relationships. Learn and practice assertive communication skills and respect others' boundaries. Healthy relationships can provide support and increase your comfort with situations that are outside of your control.

Seek Professional Help

If your obsessive control behaviors interfere with your life or cause significant distress, seek help from a mental health professional trained in CBT. They can provide additional strategies and support you in your journey toward overcoming control behaviors.

Remember, while overcoming obsessive control behaviors isn't easy, it's definitely possible. By leaning on God's strength and wisdom, utilizing CBT tools, and implementing practical strategies, you can make significant strides in releasing the need for control and embracing the freedom and peace that come from trusting in God's sovereign control.

Christian Counseling and Biblical Principles: Deepening Trust and Surrender

Surrendering Fear through Faith

It's imperative to acknowledge that fear often fuels the desire for control. Acknowledge these fears and then choose to surrender them to God, as 1 Peter 5:7 (ESV) encourages, "Cast all your anxieties on him, because he cares for you."

Cultivating a Prayerful Attitude

Develop a habit of prayer, not only as a means of presenting requests but also as a form of surrender. As Philippians 4:6 (ESV) says,

"Do not be anxious about anything, but in everything by prayer and supplication with thanksgiving let your requests be made known to God."

Engaging in Biblical Meditation

Unlike Eastern meditation, which promotes emptying the mind, biblical meditation involves filling your mind with God's Word and truths. Meditate on Scriptures that speak of God's control and care, such as Psalm 46:10 (ASV), "Be still, and know that I am God."

Encouraging Christian Fellowship

Engage regularly in fellowship with other believers who can provide a safe space to share, encourage, and pray with you. Hebrews 10:24-25 (ESV) says, "And let us consider how to stir up one another to love and good works, not neglecting to meet together."

Cognitive Behavioral Therapy (CBT) Tools and Practical Tips: Embracing Healthy Control

Understanding the Control Paradox

CBT highlights the control paradox: the more we try to control things outside of our control, the less control we feel. Accepting that there are things outside of your control can ironically make you feel more in control.

Utilizing Cognitive Defusion Techniques

Cognitive defusion techniques help you see your thoughts just as they are – thoughts, not truths or commands. This perspective can help reduce the impact of control-related thoughts.

Implementing Behavioral Experiments

Test your irrational beliefs and predictions in real-life situations. If you fear that losing control will lead to disaster, conduct small, controlled experiments to test this belief.

Developing Self-Compassion

CBT encourages developing self-compassion. Self-criticism, a common trait among people with control issues, can be mitigated by self-compassion, which promotes a healthy, balanced perspective towards oneself.

Long-Term Strategies

CBT isn't just about managing symptoms but also about fostering long-term changes in thinking and behavior patterns. By integrating these practical strategies and aligning them with biblical principles, you can create lasting changes in overcoming obsessive control behaviors.

As you navigate this journey, remember the Apostle Paul's words in 2 Corinthians 12:9-10 (ESV), "But he said to me, 'My grace is sufficient for you, for my power is made perfect in weakness.' Therefore I will boast all the more gladly of my weaknesses, so that the power of Christ may rest upon me. For the sake of Christ, then, I am content with weaknesses, insults, hardships, persecutions, and calamities. For when I am weak, then I am strong."

God's strength and wisdom, along with the practical tools from CBT, will empower you to break free from the shackles of obsessive control behaviors and experience the freedom and joy that God desires for His children.

CHAPTER 10 How Do You Get Control Over Procrastination?

Questions and Answers

Addressing procrastination often involves exploring motivations, habits, and obstacles. The following questions can be helpful in understanding and overcoming procrastination:

What tasks do you tend to procrastinate on? Identifying the tasks that are consistently put off can provide insight into why procrastination occurs.

Why do you think you procrastinate on these tasks? This can help to identify the root causes of the procrastination, which could be a lack of interest, perceived difficulty, fear of failure, or lack of clear goals.

What are the consequences of your procrastination? Understanding the negative outcomes can serve as motivation to change.

What would be the benefits of completing tasks on time? Focusing on the positive outcomes can provide additional motivation.

How do you feel when you procrastinate? Exploring the emotional state connected to procrastination can reveal whether it's being used as a coping mechanism for stress, anxiety, or other negative feelings.

What strategies have you tried to overcome procrastination? This can identify what has been attempted and what has or hasn't worked.

How do you manage your time? Do you use any tools or techniques? This could reveal potential improvements in time management that could help in reducing procrastination.

Do you set clear and achievable goals for your tasks? Clear goals can provide direction and motivation, which can help to overcome procrastination.

What activities or tasks do you prioritize over the ones you procrastinate on? This question can shed light on whether the issue is truly procrastination or if it's a matter of misaligned priorities.

Are you ready to make changes to overcome your procrastination? Change requires a commitment, and it's important to affirm readiness and willingness.

It's important to ask these questions with empathy and without judgment. Procrastination is a common behavior and can be overcome with self-awareness, effective strategies, and, in some cases, professional help.

Christian Counseling and Biblical Principles: Harnessing Proactive Stewardship

God as the Perfect Example of Diligence

We look to God as the perfect example of diligence and productivity. Genesis 2:2 (ASV) states, "And on the seventh day God finished his work which he had made; and he rested." Emulate His purposeful action in your own life.

Stewardship of Time and Talents

Recognize that time is a gift from God, and we should be good stewards of this resource. Ephesians 5:15-16 (ESV) instructs, "Look carefully then how you walk, not as unwise but as wise, making the best use of the time, because the days are evil."

Prayer and Reflection

Incorporate prayer and reflection into your daily routines. Psalm 90:12 (ASV) says, "So teach us to number our days, that we may get a heart of wisdom." Ask God for wisdom to use your time effectively and in line with His will.

Accountability Through Christian Fellowship

Find a trusted friend or group to whom you can be accountable. As Proverbs 27:17 (ESV) says, "Iron sharpens iron, and one man sharpens another." They can help you stay on track and provide encouragement when you feel overwhelmed or inclined to procrastinate.

Cognitive Behavioral Therapy (CBT) Tools and Practical Tips: Cultivating Timely Action

Understanding the Roots of Procrastination

Understand the roots of procrastination. Procrastination often comes from feelings of fear, insecurity, or perfectionism. Address these emotional barriers head-on and challenge any negative or irrational beliefs associated with them.

Implementing Behavioral Activation

Behavioral activation, a key tool in CBT, involves tackling tasks in small, manageable chunks. Instead of viewing a task as one big challenge, break it down into smaller parts and tackle them one at a time.

Practicing Mindfulness and Self-compassion

Mindfulness helps you stay focused on the present moment, while self-compassion mitigates harsh self-criticism that can fuel procrastination. Practice being kind to yourself when you're feeling overwhelmed or anxious about a task.

Visualizing Success

Visualize yourself successfully completing tasks. Visualization can help reduce anxiety and enhance motivation. Remember, it's okay not to be perfect; what's important is that you're progressing.

Creating an Action Plan

Having an action plan can provide clarity and enhance motivation. Use SMART goals (Specific, Measurable, Achievable, Relevant, Time-bound) to define what you want to achieve and the steps needed to get there.

Long-Term Strategies

Remember, overcoming procrastination is a journey, not a destination. Patience and perseverance are key, and both Christian principles and CBT provide the tools necessary to embark on this journey. Philippians 4:13 (ESV) provides a strong foundation for this journey, "I can do all things through him who strengthens me."

God's wisdom and strength, together with the practical tools from CBT, can help you overcome procrastination and achieve a more productive, fulfilling life. By cultivating diligence, accountability, and mindful action, procrastination can be replaced with purposeful, proactive stewardship.

Recognizing the Danger of Procrastination

Scripture presents numerous examples of the pitfalls of procrastination. The Parable of the Ten Virgins in Matthew 25:1-13 (ESV) underscores the dangers of being unprepared, while in Proverbs 6:6-8 (ASV), the ant's diligence stands as a rebuke to laziness. The Bible's wisdom can be an important motivator in overcoming procrastination.

Consequences of Inaction

Consider the Biblical story of Jonah, who initially ran from God's call (Jonah 1:1-3, ESV). His procrastination led to dire consequences. This story underscores the need for immediate obedience to God's guidance and the potential repercussions of delaying action.

Overcoming Fear

Many times, procrastination is rooted in fear. The story of Gideon (Judges 6-7, ESV) offers a powerful example of overcoming fear. Initially, Gideon doubted his ability to lead the Israelites against the Midianites, but with God's reassurances, he overcame his fear and proceeded with the task. Seek God's reassurances in your own life.

CBT Techniques

Cognitive Restructuring

Use cognitive restructuring to challenge and change your patterns of thinking that contribute to procrastination. You might fear failure, but remember, everyone makes mistakes. Replace the thought, "If I can't do it perfectly, I won't do it at all," with, "It's okay to make mistakes. What's important is that I try."

Self-Monitoring

Self-monitoring involves tracking your behaviors and identifying situations or feelings that trigger procrastination. With self-monitoring, you can gain insight into when and why you procrastinate, enabling you to intervene and make different choices.

Progressive Muscle Relaxation

Physical tension often accompanies feelings of anxiety or stress related to procrastination. Progressive muscle relaxation involves tensing and then releasing different muscle groups in your body, promoting physical relaxation and reducing stress.

Time Management Techniques

Creating a To-Do List

Lists can provide structure and help make tasks seem more manageable. By breaking down larger tasks into smaller steps, you can reduce feelings of being overwhelmed.

Using the Eisenhower Box

This tool helps prioritize tasks by urgency and importance, allowing you to focus on what needs to be done first and promoting effective time management.

Employing the Pomodoro Technique

The Pomodoro Technique involves working for a set amount of time (such as 25 minutes), then taking a short break (such as 5 minutes), helping maintain focus and productivity without burning out.

Balancing Work and Rest

It's important to balance work with rest. Even God rested on the seventh day (Genesis 2:2-3, ASV). Scheduling time for rest and recreation can help prevent burnout and make work periods more productive.

By merging the wisdom and strength provided by Biblical teachings and Christian fellowship with the practical, goal-oriented approach of cognitive behavioral therapy, overcoming procrastination becomes an achievable goal. Remember, change does not happen overnight. Patience, persistence, faith, and grace towards oneself are vital components of the process.

CHAPTER 11 How Do You Get Control Over Abuse of Alcohol?

Questions and Answers

Addressing alcohol abuse is a complex process, often requiring professional assistance. If you're supporting someone who's struggling with this issue, it's crucial to approach them with compassion, patience, and understanding. Here are some questions that may help guide your conversations:

1. **Can you describe your alcohol consumption?** Understanding the extent and nature of the person's drinking habits is the first step in identifying if a problem exists.

2. **Have you tried to reduce your alcohol consumption in the past?** This can provide insight into previous attempts to address the issue and potential obstacles to recovery.

3. **Are you aware of the health risks and consequences of excessive alcohol consumption?** This question helps evaluate the person's understanding of the risks involved and can serve as an opener for providing them with important information.

4. **Do you use alcohol as a means to cope with stress, emotional distress, or other problems?** Understanding the role of alcohol in the person's life can shed light on underlying issues that may be driving their alcohol abuse.

5. **Have you experienced negative consequences (personal, professional, legal, health-related) due to your alcohol consumption?** This helps to gauge the impact of alcohol abuse on their life.

6. **Do you find that you need to consume more alcohol to achieve the same effect?** This question helps determine if a physical dependence has developed.

7. **Are you willing to seek professional help for your alcohol consumption?** Overcoming alcohol abuse often requires professional intervention, and willingness to seek help is a critical step in the recovery process.

8. **How does your drinking affect your relationships with family and friends?** This can help the person understand the broader impact of their drinking habits.

9. **Do you feel that you can control your drinking or do you feel controlled by it?** This question helps evaluate their perceived locus of control over their alcohol use.

10. **Are you ready to make changes to your alcohol consumption?** The person's readiness to change is a critical factor in their recovery process.

Remember, these questions should be asked in a supportive, non-confrontational manner. If the person is ready to seek help, consider connecting them with local addiction services or a healthcare provider. For severe cases, immediate intervention may be required.

Understanding the Struggle Through a Biblical Lens

The Bible doesn't shy away from discussing the misuse of alcohol. Proverbs 20:1 (ASV) warns, "Wine is a mocker, strong drink a brawler, and whoever is led astray by it is not wise." Ephesians 5:18 (ESV) adds, "Do not get drunk with wine, for that is debauchery, but be filled with the Spirit." The Bible not only emphasizes the dangers of alcohol abuse but also provides a path towards overcoming it.

The First Step: Admitting the Problem

Recovery begins by admitting the problem, a concept mirrored in the Bible's teachings on repentance and confession. 1 John 1:9 (ESV) assures us, "If we confess our sins, he is faithful and just to forgive us our sins and to cleanse us from all unrighteousness."

Finding Strength in God

Many struggle with feelings of guilt, shame, and worthlessness due to their addiction. But the Bible reminds us of our inherent value in God's eyes and His unconditional love. In Isaiah 41:10 (ASV), God says, "Fear not, for I am with you; Be not dismayed, for I am your God; I will strengthen you, yes, I will help you."

The Role of Christian Community

The Christian community can provide significant support in overcoming alcohol addiction. Galatians 6:2 (ESV) implores us to "Bear one another's burdens, and so fulfill the law of Christ." Seek out a supportive, non-judgmental community, such as a local church or Christian recovery group.

CBT Techniques for Overcoming Alcohol Abuse

Understanding the ABCs of CBT

In CBT, the "ABC" model helps to understand the connection between thoughts (A - Antecedents), behaviors (B - Behaviors), and consequences (C - Consequences). By identifying and changing negative thought patterns that lead to alcohol misuse, you can change the behaviors and thus the consequences.

Mindfulness and Sobriety

Mindfulness, a core component of CBT, can be a powerful tool in maintaining sobriety. By cultivating an awareness of the present moment without judgment, you can better manage cravings and recognize triggers.

Coping Skills Training

This CBT technique helps develop effective strategies to deal with stressors and triggers for alcohol use. These skills can include distraction techniques, relaxation exercises, and problem-solving strategies.

Relapse Prevention

CBT's relapse prevention strategies focus on identifying high-risk situations, developing coping mechanisms, and creating a detailed plan for preventing and dealing with relapses.

Finding Your Values

In CBT, clarifying one's values can be an important aspect of recovery. When you're clear about what matters most to you, it's easier to make decisions that align with those values, including the decision to abstain from alcohol.

Creating a Balanced Life

A vital part of recovery is creating a balanced, fulfilling life. This can involve setting and working towards personal goals, developing healthy relationships, and engaging in activities that bring joy and satisfaction.

Restoration through God's Love and Mercy

As you begin your journey to overcome alcohol abuse, remember to lean on God's mercy and grace. Lamentations 3:22-23 (ASV) encourages us, "The Lord's loving kindnesses indeed never cease, for His compassions never fail. They are new every morning; great is Your faithfulness." Each day presents an opportunity for restoration, a chance to draw closer to God's love and experience His merciful compassion.

Reflection and Repentance

Continual reflection and repentance are key in the journey to overcome alcohol abuse. Acts 3:19 (ESV) advises, "Repent, then, and turn to God, so that your sins may be wiped out, that times of refreshing may come from the Lord." Regular prayer and meditation, seeking God's wisdom and strength, can foster deep inner change.

Abiding in Christ

One of the most profound ways to overcome alcohol abuse is to continually abide in Christ, as counseled in John 15:4 (ESV): "Abide in me, and I in you." The daily practice of reading and studying scripture, praying, and seeking God's presence can fuel your strength to overcome this challenge.

Finding Joy in the Lord

The Bible urges us to seek our joy in the Lord rather than earthly pleasures. In Nehemiah 8:10 (ASV), we read, "The joy of the Lord is your strength." Replacing the temporary pleasure of alcohol with the enduring joy found in a relationship with God can be a powerful tool in your journey towards sobriety.

Cognitive-Behavioral Therapy (CBT) Techniques

Recognizing Cognitive Distortions

CBT often involves identifying cognitive distortions, which are inaccurate thoughts that can lead to unhealthy emotional states and behaviors. For instance, you might believe "I can't have fun without alcohol" or "I can't cope with stress without drinking." Recognizing these distortions is the first step towards correcting them.

Cognitive Restructuring

Once you've identified cognitive distortions, cognitive restructuring can help you challenge and change these unhealthy thought patterns. For example, you can replace the thought "I need alcohol to relax" with "There are many ways I can relax without alcohol, like reading a book, taking a walk, or practicing deep breathing."

Behavioral Experiments

In CBT, you might also engage in behavioral experiments to test the validity of your thoughts and beliefs. For example, if you believe you can't enjoy a social event without drinking, you might attend a gathering and commit to staying sober. This can provide first-hand evidence that challenges and ultimately changes your beliefs about alcohol.

Self-Monitoring

Self-monitoring involves tracking your thoughts, feelings, and behaviors related to alcohol use. By keeping a journal of when and why you drink, you can start to identify patterns and triggers. This can inform your coping strategies and help you anticipate and manage high-risk situations.

Developing Healthy Coping Mechanisms

CBT also focuses on developing healthy coping mechanisms to deal with stress and negative emotions. This can involve learning relaxation techniques, improving problem-solving skills, and engaging in physical activities, among others.

Remember, it's essential to seek professional help when overcoming alcohol abuse. A professional can provide a tailored treatment plan and provide support throughout your journey. Coupled with your faith and commitment, these tools can help you break free from alcohol abuse and find greater fulfillment in a life guided by God's love and wisdom.

With the combination of Biblical wisdom, Christian fellowship, and CBT techniques, overcoming alcohol abuse is possible. However, it's important to remember that recovery is a process, not an event. It involves patience, persistence, grace, and a lot of hard work. But with the right tools and support, you can turn old habits into new ones and live a life free from the grip of alcohol.

CHAPTER 12 How Do You Get Control Overeating?

Questions and Answers

When seeking to understand and help someone overcome overeating, it's crucial to approach the situation with compassion and understanding. Here are some questions that may be helpful:

1. **Can you describe your eating habits?** Understanding the nature and pattern of someone's eating habits is the first step to identifying the issue.

2. **Are there particular foods that you find hard to resist or eat in moderation?** Some individuals may struggle with specific types of food, often high in sugar or fat.

3. **Do you often eat when you're not physically hungry?** This question can help identify emotional eating, where individuals use food to cope with feelings.

4. **Are there specific situations, emotions, or triggers that lead you to overeat?** Stress, boredom, or certain environments can trigger overeating.

5. **How do you feel before, during, and after you overeat?** These feelings can provide insight into what drives the behavior and the consequences that follow.

6. **How does overeating affect your physical and emotional well-being?** Understanding the impact on their well-being can help motivate change.

7. **Have you tried to control your eating habits in the past? What worked, and what didn't?** This can help identify potential strategies for managing overeating.

8. **What role does food play in your life?** For some people, food might serve as comfort, reward, or a way to deal with emotions.

9. **Are you ready to make changes to your eating habits?** Their readiness to change is a critical factor in their potential for overcoming overeating.

10. **Would you consider seeking professional help, such as a registered dietitian or a psychologist specializing in eating disorders?** Professional from a Christian counselor can help can provide effective strategies and support in dealing with overeating.

These questions should be asked in a supportive, non-judgmental manner, as it's important for the individual to feel safe and understood. Keep in mind that overcoming overeating often involves addressing both physical and emotional aspects and may require the help of professionals.

Biblical and Christian Counseling

Understanding the Underlying Issue: Idolatry

Oftentimes, overeating stems from something much deeper: a heart issue. Paul says in Philippians 3:19, "Their end is destruction, their god is their belly, and they glory in their shame, with minds set on earthly things." The original Greek word for "belly" here is "koilia," which is more than just our physical stomach; it implies the desires and appetites of our sinful nature. Here, overeating is seen as a form of idolatry – placing the satisfaction of our appetites above our obedience and reverence to God. This perspective is not meant to shame, but rather to bring to light the root issue that needs to be addressed.

The Call to Self-Control

One of the fruits of the Spirit outlined by Paul in Galatians 5:22-23 is self-control (Greek: "egkrateia"). This term derives from the root word "kratos," meaning "strength," and the prefix "en," meaning "in." Therefore, "egkrateia" implies a strength or mastery from within. This mastery is not self-generated but is a fruit produced by the Holy Spirit within us. A person with "egkrateia" isn't controlled by their desires but has mastery over them.

The Principle of Stewardship

Our bodies are not our own; they are a gift from God. We are called to be stewards of our bodies, as illustrated in 1 Corinthians 6:19-20, "Or do you not know that your body is a temple of the Holy Spirit within you, whom you have from God? You are not your own, for you were bought with a price. So glorify God in your body." The term "temple" (Greek: "naos") indicates a sacred place, signifying that our bodies are sacred spaces for God's Spirit. This recognition can motivate us to treat our bodies with respect and care, making healthier eating choices as an act of worship.

Cognitive Behavioral Therapy (CBT)

Mindful Eating

In cognitive-behavioral therapy, one approach to control overeating is the practice of mindful eating. This technique involves paying full attention to the experience of eating, noting the colors, smells, textures, and tastes of food. It encourages you to eat slowly, savoring each bite, which can help you better recognize your body's hunger and fullness cues, reducing the likelihood of overeating.

Identifying and Challenging Negative Thought Patterns

CBT emphasizes the role of cognitions (thoughts) in shaping our behavior. People who struggle with overeating often harbor negative, self-defeating thoughts such as "I'll never be able to control my eating" or "I've already blown my diet for today, so I might as well keep eating." CBT teaches you to identify these thought patterns and challenge their accuracy. The more you practice this skill, the more you can foster healthier, more balanced thoughts that promote better eating behaviors.

Developing Coping Skills

Overeating is often a coping mechanism for stress, anxiety, or other negative emotions. CBT can help you develop healthier coping skills, such as deep breathing, progressive muscle relaxation, or engaging in a hobby. The goal is to offer alternative responses to emotional triggers, reducing the reliance on food for comfort.

Building Self-Efficacy

CBT also focuses on building self-efficacy - your belief in your ability to succeed in specific situations. Therapists might encourage clients to set achievable goals for healthier eating and exercise, providing a framework for small, sustainable changes. As these changes accumulate, they can significantly impact eating behaviors and body weight, fostering a greater sense of self-efficacy.

It is critical to remember that overcoming overeating, like other habits, is a journey, not a destination. It involves ongoing learning, unlearning, and relearning. There may be setbacks, but they do not denote failure, but rather opportunities for growth and learning. With the help of biblical principles, Christian counseling, and CBT, you can gain control overeating and cultivate a healthier relationship with food.

CHAPTER 13 How Do You Get Control Over Your Smoking Cigarettes?

Questions and Answers

Helping someone overcome cigarette smoking can be a challenging task, as it often involves addressing both physical addiction and behavioral habits. Here are some questions that could guide your conversation:

1. **Can you describe your smoking habits?** Understanding how often and when they smoke can help identify patterns and triggers.

2. **What situations or feelings usually trigger your need to smoke?** Triggers could be stress, social situations, after meals, or when drinking alcohol.

3. **Have you tried to quit smoking before? What worked and what didn't?** Previous attempts can provide insights into what strategies might be effective or ineffective.

4. **What are your main reasons for wanting to quit smoking?** These can be used as motivations during the quitting process.

5. **Are you aware of the health risks associated with smoking?** Understanding the potential health risks can be a significant motivator.

6. **How does smoking impact your daily life and relationships?** This question can help them realize the broader impact of their smoking habit.

7. **Do you believe you can quit smoking?** This can gauge their self-efficacy, which is important for motivation and success in quitting.

8. **Are you ready to cope with withdrawal symptoms that might come with quitting?** This helps them prepare for the challenges they may face when they stop smoking.
9. **Would you consider seeking professional help or support groups?** These can provide strategies, resources, and support to increase the chance of success.
10. **Are you open to using smoking cessation aids such as nicotine replacement therapy or prescription medications?** There are several proven methods that can assist in the quitting process.

These questions should be asked in a supportive and non-judgmental manner. It's important to remember that overcoming addiction to cigarettes often requires multiple attempts, patience, and a lot of support. Professional help can significantly enhance the chance of successful cessation.

Christian Counseling and Biblical Principles

Understanding the Implications of Your Habits

The Apostle Paul wrote in 1 Corinthians 6:19-20, "Or do you not know that your body is a temple of the Holy Spirit within you, whom you have from God? You are not your own, for you were bought with a price. So glorify God in your body." The Greek word for temple here is "naos," which signifies a dwelling place of God. This indicates that we must strive to keep our bodies, including our lungs, clean and pure, as a way of showing reverence and obedience to God.

Surrender to God's Will

Romans 12:2 implores us, "Do not be conformed to this world, but be transformed by the renewal (anakainōsis) of your mind, that by testing you may discern what is the will of God, what is good and acceptable and perfect." Here, Paul encourages us to replace our harmful habits, like smoking, with habits that are more pleasing to God. The word "anakainōsis" implies a thorough change for the better. Thus, the call is not just to quit smoking, but to replace it with healthier habits, so that we can live out God's will in a healthier body and mind.

Practice Self-Control

One of the fruits of the Spirit that Paul describes in Galatians 5:22-23 is self-control (egkrateia). This concept implies having power or dominion from within, over our desires and passions. A key aspect of quitting smoking is developing self-control over our cravings for cigarettes, and this self-control is something that the Spirit can produce within us as we grow in our relationship with God.

Cognitive Behavioral Therapy (CBT) Approach

Identify Triggers

CBT helps you identify the triggers that lead you to smoke. These can be situations, feelings, or thoughts that make you want to light a cigarette. Once you've identified these triggers, you can start to plan how to handle these situations or feelings without resorting to smoking.

Cognitive Restructuring

This involves changing the way you think about smoking. For example, instead of thinking "I need a cigarette to relax," you might start telling yourself "Taking a deep breath or going for a walk can help me relax." By changing these thought patterns, you can decrease your desire to smoke.

Behavioral Strategies

CBT offers several behavioral strategies for quitting smoking. One popular method is the "delay" technique. When you get the urge to smoke, delay it for 5, 10, 15 minutes, or longer, with the hope that the craving will pass. Other strategies include avoiding situations where you usually smoke, or changing your routine to disrupt smoking habits.

Building Self-Efficacy

CBT helps build your confidence in your ability to quit smoking. This can be achieved through small victories like resisting a craving, going a day without a cigarette, or overcoming a trigger situation without smoking. Celebrating these victories can boost your self-efficacy, increasing your belief in your ability to quit for good.

Ultimately, quitting smoking requires a mix of spiritual growth and practical strategies. By drawing on biblical principles and CBT techniques, you can find the strength and resources to overcome this habit, leading to a healthier and more fulfilling life.

CHAPTER 14 How Do You Get Control Over Your Spending Too Much Time on Social Media?

Questions and Answers

Addressing the issue of spending too much time on social media involves understanding the reasons behind the behavior, its impacts, and readiness to change. Here are some questions that can help guide your conversation:

1. **How much time do you spend on social media each day?** This question can help you and the person quantify the extent of the problem.

2. **Which platforms do you spend the most time on and what are you usually doing?** This can help identify patterns and what aspects of social media usage are most time-consuming.

3. **Do you feel that your use of social media interferes with your work, studies, or personal life?** Understanding the impacts can help motivate change.

4. **Are there certain times or situations when you tend to use social media more?** Identifying triggers can be useful in developing strategies to manage the behavior.

5. **Have you tried to reduce your social media use in the past? What strategies did you use and how successful were they?** This provides insights into what methods might work for the individual.

6. **How do you feel when you're not able to use social media?** Feelings of anxiety or restlessness can indicate a psychological dependency.

7. **Do you use social media to escape from or cope with negative feelings or stressful situations?** This could suggest that social media is being used as a coping mechanism.
8. **What benefits do you perceive from using social media?** Understanding the perceived benefits can help in finding healthier alternatives that provide similar benefits.
9. **Are you ready to make changes to your social media usage?** Readiness to change is a critical factor in success.
10. **Would you consider seeking professional help, if needed?** If social media use is seriously impacting their life, professional help may be necessary.

These questions should be asked in a non-judgmental and supportive manner. It's important to remember that changing habits takes time, patience, and a lot of understanding.

Christian Counseling and Biblical Principles

The Principle of Moderation and Self-Control

In Philippians 4:5, Paul tells us to "Let your reasonableness be known to everyone." The Greek word for reasonableness is "epieikes," meaning mildness, gentleness, or moderation. This suggests that our interactions with the world, including our use of social media, should be characterized by restraint and balance.

In Galatians 5:22-23, the Bible speaks about the fruit of the Spirit, one of which is self-control (egkrateia), implying having power or dominion from within. In the context of social media, exercising self-control means setting reasonable limits on our usage to prevent it from interfering with other essential areas of life like relationships, work, or spiritual development.

The Value of Time

Ephesians 5:15-16 encourages us to "Look carefully then how you walk, not as unwise but as wise, making the best use of the time, because the days are evil." The phrase "making the best use of the time" in Greek is "exagorazomenoi ton kairon," which means redeeming or buying up the opportunity. This principle suggests that time is a precious commodity that we should use wisely. Spending excessive time on social media often results in missed opportunities for more enriching and fulfilling activities.

Guarding our Minds

Philippians 4:8 instructs us to think about things that are true, honorable, just, pure, lovely, commendable, excellent, and praiseworthy. The Greek word for think is "logizomai," which implies a deep, deliberate meditation or consideration. Given the plethora of content on social media, not all of it aligns with these characteristics. Therefore, it's vital to guard our minds and make deliberate choices about what content we consume.

Cognitive Behavioral Therapy (CBT) Approach

Digital Detox

CBT recommends taking regular breaks from social media or going for a complete digital detox for a set period. This technique can help reset your relationship with social media, making you more aware of the amount of time you spend on it, and how it impacts your mental health and productivity.

Cognitive Restructuring

CBT encourages the identification and challenging of irrational thoughts that fuel excessive social media use. For example, the belief that "I'll miss out on something important if I don't check my social media frequently" can be challenged and replaced with a more rational thought like, "It's unlikely that anything critical will happen if I don't check social media for a few hours."

Behavioral Activation

Instead of spending excessive time on social media, CBT encourages individuals to engage in other fulfilling and meaningful activities. By scheduling these activities and following through, individuals can gradually replace the time spent on social media with these healthier alternatives.

Mindfulness

Mindfulness involves staying present and fully engaged in the current activity without being distracted by social media. It helps individuals realize the amount of time they are wasting and the negative impact it has on their mental well-being.

In summary, while social media can be a valuable tool for connecting with others and staying informed, it's important to use it wisely and in moderation. By integrating biblical principles with CBT techniques, individuals can maintain a healthy relationship with social media, ensuring it enriches rather than consumes their lives.

CHAPTER 15 How Do You Get Control Over Being Overly Critical or Negative Towards Others?

Questions and Answers

Helping someone address being overly critical or negative towards others requires understanding their motivations and providing them with strategies to change their behavior. Here are some questions that can guide the conversation:

1. **Can you identify situations where you find yourself being overly critical or negative?** This can help the person identify patterns or triggers.

2. **How do you feel when you're being critical or negative towards others?** This question can help them identify emotions that might be driving their behavior.

3. **What impact does your criticism or negativity have on your relationships?** Understanding the consequences can provide motivation to change.

4. **Have you received feedback about your critical or negative behavior from others?** Feedback can provide valuable insight into how others perceive their behavior.

5. **Do you feel there are more constructive ways you could express your opinions or concerns?** This question can help them identify alternative ways of communicating.

6. **Are there any underlying feelings or issues that might be contributing to your behavior?** Understanding the root causes can be crucial in addressing the problem.

7. **What strategies have you tried to manage your critical or negative behavior?** This can help identify what has been attempted and what has or hasn't worked.
8. **Do you think your expectations of others are realistic?** This can help the person assess if they are holding others to an unreasonably high standard.
9. **Are you ready to make changes in your behavior?** Their readiness to change is a critical factor in the process.
10. **Would you consider seeking professional help such as therapy or coaching?** These professionals can provide effective strategies and tools for managing behavior and improving communication.

These questions should be asked in a supportive and non-confrontational manner. It's also important to remember that changing behavior takes time and patience, and often requires professional help.

Christian Counseling and Biblical Principles

The Power of the Tongue

Proverbs 18:21 (ASV) reads, "Death and life are in the power of the tongue." This principle implies that our words hold immense power. They can build up and bring life or tear down and bring harm. It's crucial, then, that we temper our speech, especially when it comes to criticism. Being overly critical or negative can often do more harm than good, even when our intentions might be constructive.

The Principle of Love and Kindness

Ephesians 4:32 (ESV) instructs, "Be kind to one another, tenderhearted, forgiving one another, as God in Christ forgave you." Here, "tenderhearted" translates the Greek "eusplagchnos," meaning having strong compassion or being of a compassionate nature. This suggests that when dealing with others, our words and actions should be driven by kindness, empathy, and understanding, not harshness and negativity.

The Call to Encourage and Build Each Other Up

In 1 Thessalonians 5:11 (ESV), Paul writes, "Therefore encourage one another and build one another up, just as you are doing." The word for "build" in Greek is "oikodomeo," which means to construct or improve a building. Applied metaphorically, it's an encouragement to contribute to someone's growth and betterment. This requires us to balance criticism with a lot of encouragement, advice, and positive feedback.

Judge Not, That You Be Not Judged

Matthew 7:1 (ESV) warns us, "Judge not, that you be not judged." This verse highlights the danger of being overly critical or judgmental. When we constantly criticize others, we expose ourselves to the same level of scrutiny and judgment.

Cognitive Behavioral Therapy (CBT) Approach

Cognitive Restructuring

Overly critical behavior often stems from cognitive distortions like overgeneralization, magnifying negatives, minimizing positives, and jumping to conclusions. CBT helps individuals identify these distortions and replace them with more rational thoughts. For instance, the thought, "They're always messing up," can be changed to, "They made a mistake this time, but they also do many things well."

Practicing Empathy

CBT encourages developing empathy as a counterbalance to critical behavior. This involves trying to understand others' perspectives and experiences, which can soften harsh judgments and criticisms.

Mindfulness and Self-Awareness

Mindfulness helps increase self-awareness, enabling individuals to recognize when they're being overly critical or negative. They can then choose to pause and reframe their thoughts in a more constructive and kinder way.

Communication Skills Training

CBT also emphasizes learning effective communication skills. Being able to express thoughts and feelings respectfully and assertively, rather than critically, can improve relationships significantly.

Developing a Positive Attitude

CBT encourages individuals to cultivate a positive attitude. This includes focusing on positives, practicing gratitude, and adopting an optimistic mindset. Over time, this can help reduce critical and negative behavior.

Living in Light of God's Grace

Romans 3:23 (ESV) affirms, "For all have sinned and fall short of the glory of God." As we reflect on this universal truth, we are reminded of our own flaws and limitations. This is not to promote a sense of self-deprecation, but rather to instill humility. Recognizing that we too are not perfect, we should extend grace to others as God has extended grace to us. Remember the Greek word "hamartano," meaning "to miss the mark." Just as we sometimes miss the mark in our own lives, so do others. It's through this lens of grace that we can begin to soften our critical attitudes.

Modeling Christ's Humility and Consideration for Others

Philippians 2:3-4 (ESV) urges, "Do nothing from selfish ambition or conceit, but in humility count others more significant than yourselves. Let each of you look not only to his own interests, but also to the interests of others." Emulating Christ's humility and selflessness, we can learn to value others and their viewpoints. As we internalize these principles, we will naturally become less critical and more accepting.

Cognitive Behavioral Therapy (CBT) Approach

Self-Compassion Practices

Overly critical individuals often direct their criticism inward, fostering a harsh inner critic. CBT incorporates self-compassion practices to counter this, encouraging individuals to treat themselves with the same kindness they would extend to a friend. By nurturing self-compassion, it becomes easier to extend compassion to others, softening critical attitudes.

Behavioral Experiments

CBT employs behavioral experiments to challenge and change overly critical attitudes. This could involve setting tasks that encourage individuals to act contrary to their negative beliefs about others, observing the outcomes, and using these experiences to inform more balanced views. For instance, if a person believes others are always incompetent, they might delegate an important task and discover that it's executed successfully.

Assertiveness Training

Being overly critical can sometimes be a misguided form of assertiveness. CBT assertiveness training involves teaching individuals to express their needs and desires in a respectful, balanced way, without resorting to harsh criticism or negativity.

Balancing Criticism with Praise

In both Christian counseling and CBT, it's vital to balance criticism with praise. Proverbs 16:24 (ASV) suggests, "Pleasant words are as a honeycomb, Sweet to the soul, and health to the bones." Pleasant words - words of encouragement, affirmation, and appreciation - are essential in cultivating positive interactions.

In the context of CBT, this could involve a conscious effort to praise more than criticize, thereby changing the negative communication pattern. For instance, for every criticism, aim to give five compliments. Over time, this can help shift a hypercritical focus towards a more balanced perspective.

Remember, both Christian counseling and CBT are not quick fixes but involve a process of continual growth and development. Combining the timeless wisdom of the Bible and the practical strategies of CBT, individuals can progressively overcome overly critical and negative attitudes, fostering healthier interactions with themselves and others.

In sum, overcoming a tendency to be overly critical or negative involves a combination of adopting biblical principles of love, kindness, and careful speech, as well as employing CBT strategies such as cognitive restructuring, empathy, mindfulness, and effective communication. This approach allows for a deeper and more sustainable transformation.

CHAPTER 16 How Do You Get Control Over Gossiping?

Questions and Answers

How damaging is malicious gossip, or slander?

According to the Bible, malicious gossip and slander are highly damaging and are considered sinful. Scripture provides clear warnings about the harmful effects of such behavior and emphasizes the importance of guarding our speech.

In Proverbs 18:21 (ESV), it is stated, "Death and life are in the power of the tongue, and those who love it will eat its fruits." This verse underscores the significant impact our words can have, either bringing life and edification or causing destruction and harm. Malicious gossip and slander fall into the latter category, leading to broken relationships, damaged reputations, and emotional pain.

Additionally, the Bible condemns false and deceitful speech. Proverbs 12:22 (ESV) declares, "Lying lips are an abomination to the Lord, but those who act faithfully are his delight." Slanderous gossip often involves spreading falsehoods or distorting the truth, which goes against God's desire for honesty and integrity.

In the New Testament, the apostle Paul instructs believers to put away falsehood and speak the truth. Ephesians 4:25 (ESV) states, "Therefore, having put away falsehood, let each one of you speak the truth with his neighbor, for we are members one of another." This command encompasses not only avoiding direct lies but also refraining from spreading false information or engaging in slanderous speech about others.

Furthermore, Jesus Himself warned about the accountability we have for our words. In Matthew 12:36-37 (ESV), He said, "I tell you, on the day of judgment people will give account for every careless word they speak, for by your words you will be justified, and by your words, you will be condemned." This serves as a sobering reminder that our speech holds weight in God's sight and will be evaluated when we stand before Him.

What is the difference between gossip and slander?

In biblical terms, gossip and slander are related but distinct concepts, although they are often intertwined. Understanding their differences can help us navigate our speech in a manner that aligns with biblical principles.

Gossip generally refers to casual or idle talk about the personal affairs of others. It involves sharing information about someone else, often without their knowledge or consent, and discussing their actions, circumstances, or character. Gossip can encompass both positive and negative information, but it becomes harmful when it involves spreading rumors, unverified information, or engaging in conversation that tears down or damages someone's reputation. Gossip typically involves sharing details about others' lives that may not be necessary or edifying for those involved in the conversation.

Slander, on the other hand, is a more specific form of harmful speech. It involves making false, damaging, or malicious statements about someone, often with the intention of causing harm or tarnishing their reputation. Slander typically includes spreading false information or accusations that can lead to the defamation of another person's character. Slanderous statements can cause significant harm to the individual's reputation, relationships, and overall well-being.

In biblical terms, both gossip and slander are seen as detrimental to individuals and communities. Proverbs 20:19 (ESV) warns, "Whoever goes about slandering reveals secrets; therefore do not associate with a simple babbler." This verse highlights the harmful nature of both gossip and slander, emphasizing the need to distance oneself from those who engage in such behavior.

What is the essence of Paul's counsel at 1 Timothy 5:11-15?

The counsel given by Paul in 1 Timothy 5:11-15 addresses the issue of younger widows in the church community. Let's explore the essence of Paul's counsel in this passage, highlighting important Scripture references and providing additional insights.

Context and Background Before delving into the specific verses, it's essential to understand the context of Paul's letter to Timothy. The apostle Paul wrote 1 Timothy to provide guidance and instructions to Timothy, a young leader in the early Christian community. The letter covers various topics related to church leadership, conduct, and the proper functioning of the Christian congregation.

1 Timothy 5:11-15 Let's examine the key verses that contain Paul's counsel:

"11 But refuse to enroll younger widows, for when their passions draw them away from Christ, they desire to marry 12 and so incur condemnation for having abandoned their former faith. 13 Besides that, they learn to be idlers, going about from house to house, and not only idlers but also gossips and busybodies, saying what they should not. 14 So I would have younger widows marry, bear children, manage their households, and give the adversary no occasion for slander. 15 For some have already strayed after Satan." (1 Timothy 5:11-15, ESV)

Counsel to Refrain from Enrolling Younger Widows In these verses, Paul advises against enrolling younger widows into a formal support program within the church community. The reasons behind this counsel are twofold:

1. **Passions and Desire for Marriage**: Paul highlights that younger widows may be prone to having their passions draw them away from Christ and desiring to remarry (1 Timothy 5:11-12). By encouraging marriage, Paul aims to guide them toward a stable family life and away from potential spiritual pitfalls.

2. **Negative Behaviors**: Paul further warns about the potential negative consequences of idleness among younger widows (1 Timothy 5:13). Idle widows may become gossips, spreading harmful information, and busybodies, involving themselves in other people's affairs unnecessarily. These behaviors can be detrimental to the unity and reputation of the Christian community.

Recommendation for Marriage and Family Life Instead of enrolling younger widows, Paul advises that they marry, bear children, manage their households, and give no occasion for slander (1 Timothy 5:14). This counsel emphasizes the importance of fulfilling family responsibilities and focusing on maintaining a positive reputation. By doing so, they protect themselves from falling into idleness, gossip, and negative behaviors that can harm their witness and the community.

Guarding Against Spiritual Straying Paul concludes this section by noting that some younger widows have already strayed after Satan (1 Timothy 5:15). This highlights the potential spiritual dangers associated with neglecting proper responsibilities and engaging in harmful behaviors.

Insights from Original Language While the original Greek terms in this passage do not carry significant additional layers of meaning, understanding the context and broader teachings of Scripture helps illuminate the counsel provided. The specific words used in these verses convey the importance of avoiding negative behaviors and pursuing godly conduct within the church community.

What should be done to overcome a personal weakness for the type of gossiping that may lead to slander?

Recognize the Need for Change and Seek God's Help

The first step in overcoming a personal weakness for gossiping that may lead to slander is to recognize the need for change and acknowledge that this behavior is not aligned with God's standards.

This self-awareness and conviction prompt us to seek God's help in transforming our hearts and minds.

Scriptural Support:

- Psalm 139:23-24 (ESV): "Search me, O God, and know my heart! Try me and know my thoughts! And see if there be any grievous way in me, and lead me in the way everlasting."
- James 1:19 (ESV): "Know this, my beloved brothers: let every person be quick to hear, slow to speak, slow to anger."

Renew Your Mind and Focus on Truth

Overcoming a weakness for gossip and slander requires renewing our minds and aligning our thoughts with God's truth. We must fill our minds with positive and edifying thoughts, replacing gossip with words that build up others and honor God.

Scriptural Support:

- Romans 12:2 (ESV): "Do not be conformed to this world, but be transformed by the renewal of your mind, that by testing you may discern what is the will of God, what is good and acceptable and perfect."
- Philippians 4:8 (ESV): "Finally, brothers, whatever is true, whatever is honorable, whatever is just, whatever is pure, whatever is lovely, whatever is commendable, if there is any excellence, if there is anything worthy of praise, think about these things."

Exercise Self-Control and Guard Your Tongue

Developing self-control and guarding our tongues are crucial steps in overcoming the tendency to engage in harmful gossip. We must learn to restrain our speech, refrain from spreading harmful information, and redirect conversations in a positive and uplifting direction.

Scriptural Support:

- Proverbs 10:19 (ESV): "When words are many, transgression is not lacking, but whoever restrains his lips is prudent."

- James 3:5-6 (ESV): "So also the tongue is a small member, yet it boasts of great things. How great a forest is set ablaze by such a small fire! And the tongue is a fire, a world of unrighteousness. The tongue is set among our members, staining the whole body, setting on fire the entire course of life, and set on fire by hell."

Seek Accountability and Surround Yourself with Supportive Community

Accountability and supportive community play a significant role in overcoming personal weaknesses. Seek out trusted individuals who can hold you accountable, encourage you to change, and provide guidance and support along the way.

Scriptural Support:

- Proverbs 27:17 (ESV): "Iron sharpens iron, and one man sharpens another."
- Hebrews 10:24-25 (ESV): "And let us consider how to stir up one another to love and good works, not neglecting to meet together, as is the habit of some, but encouraging one another, and all the more as you see the Day drawing near."

Pray for Transformation and Practice Forgiveness

Prayer is a powerful tool in seeking transformation. We should pray earnestly for God's guidance, strength, and grace to overcome our weaknesses. Additionally, practicing forgiveness is crucial, both for ourselves and for others, as we navigate the journey of growth and change.

Scriptural Support:

- Philippians 4:6-7 (ESV): "Do not be anxious about anything, but in everything by prayer and supplication with thanksgiving let your requests be made known to God. And the peace of God, which surpasses all understanding, will guard your hearts and your minds in Christ Jesus."
- Matthew 6:14-15 (ESV): "For if you forgive others their trespasses, your heavenly Father will also forgive you, but if

you do not forgive others their trespasses, neither will your Father forgive your trespasses."

By implementing these principles, seeking God's help, and cultivating a heart transformed by His truth and love, we can overcome the personal weakness for gossiping that may lead to slander. Remember, this is a continual process that requires diligence and dependence on God's grace and transforming power.

Scripturally, why would you say that all of us should control what we say?

The Power of Words and Their Impact

Scripturally, there are compelling reasons why all of us should control what we say. The Bible emphasizes the power of words and their significant impact on our lives and the lives of others. Understanding and harnessing this power is crucial for our relationships, spiritual growth, and overall well-being.

Scriptural Support:

- Proverbs 18:21 (ASV): "Death and life are in the power of the tongue, and those who love it will eat its fruits."
- Proverbs 12:18 (ESV): "There is one whose rash words are like sword thrusts, but the tongue of the wise brings healing."

Reflecting Our Inner Nature

What we say is a reflection of our inner nature and heart condition. Our words reveal the state of our hearts and can impact how others perceive us. Controlling what we say allows us to align our speech with God's standards and demonstrate His love and grace through our words.

Scriptural Support:

- Matthew 12:34-35 (ESV): "For out of the abundance of the heart the mouth speaks. The good person out of his good treasure brings forth good, and the evil person out of his evil treasure brings forth evil."

- Luke 6:45 (ESV): "The good person out of the good treasure of his heart produces good, and the evil person out of his evil treasure produces evil, for out of the abundance of the heart his mouth speaks."

Building Up Others and Edifying Speech

Controlling what we say enables us to use our words to build up and encourage others. Our speech should be characterized by kindness, love, and edification. By exercising control over our words, we can contribute to positive and uplifting communication within our relationships and communities.

Scriptural Support:

- Ephesians 4:29 (ASV): "Let no corrupting talk come out of your mouths, but only such as is good for building up, as fits the occasion, that it may give grace to those who hear."
- Proverbs 16:24 (ESV): "Gracious words are like a honeycomb, sweetness to the soul and health to the body."

Avoiding Harm and Conflict

Controlling what we say helps us avoid causing harm and conflict through our words. Words spoken without thought or in anger can have lasting consequences and damage relationships. By exercising self-control over our speech, we can promote peace, reconciliation, and harmony in our interactions with others.

Scriptural Support:

- Proverbs 17:27 (ESV): "Whoever restrains his words has knowledge, and he who has a cool spirit is a man of understanding."
- James 3:5-6 (ESV): "So also the tongue is a small member, yet it boasts of great things. How great a forest is set ablaze by such a small fire! And the tongue is a fire, a world of unrighteousness. The tongue is set among our members, staining the whole body, setting on fire the entire course of life, and set on fire by hell."

Honoring God and Living in Obedience

Controlling what we say is an act of obedience and reverence towards God. It aligns with His commandments to speak truth, avoid falsehood, and use our words for His glory. Our speech should reflect the character of Christ and honor God in all that we say.

Scriptural Support:

- Psalm 19:14 (ASV): "Let the words of my mouth and the meditation of my heart be acceptable in your sight, O Lord, my rock and my redeemer."

- Colossians 3:17 (ESV): "And whatever you do, in word or deed, do everything in the name of the Lord Jesus, giving thanks to God the Father through him."

By recognizing the power of words, reflecting our inner nature, building up others, avoiding harm and conflict, and honoring God, we understand the scriptural reasons why we should control what we say. Through the guidance of the Holy Spirit and a commitment to aligning our speech with God's Word, we can experience transformation in our communication and bring glory to God.

Why is it not always wrong to talk about fellow Christians?

Talking about Fellow Christians: The Context and Purpose

While gossip and slander are condemned in the Bible, it is not always wrong to talk about fellow Christians. The context and purpose of the conversation play a significant role in determining the appropriateness of discussing others. Scripture provides guidance on when and how to talk about fellow believers in ways that are beneficial and aligned with God's principles.

Scriptural Support:

- Ephesians 4:29 (ESV): "Let no corrupting talk come out of your mouths, but only such as is good for building up, as fits the occasion, that it may give grace to those who hear."

- Colossians 4:6 (ESV): "Let your speech always be gracious, seasoned with salt, so that you may know how you ought to answer each person."

Informative and Edifying Communication

Talking about fellow Christians can be appropriate and beneficial when it involves informative and edifying communication. Sharing important updates, achievements, prayer requests, and testimonies can foster a sense of community, encourage support, and promote unity among believers.

Scriptural Support:

- Ephesians 6:21-22 (ESV): "So that you also may know how I am and what I am doing, Tychicus the beloved brother and faithful minister in the Lord will tell you everything. I have sent him to you for this very purpose, that you may know how we are, and that he may encourage your hearts."
- Colossians 4:8-9 (ESV): "I have sent him to you for this very purpose, that you may know how we are and that he may encourage your hearts, and with him Onesimus, our faithful and beloved brother, who is one of you. They will tell you of everything that has taken place here."

Seeking Guidance, Support, and Accountability

Talking about fellow Christians can also be appropriate when seeking guidance, support, and accountability within the body of believers. Sharing struggles, seeking wise counsel, and engaging in mutual edification contribute to spiritual growth and strengthening of the community.

Scriptural Support:

- Proverbs 27:17 (ASV): "Iron sharpeneth iron; So a man sharpeneth the countenance of his friend."
- James 5:16 (ESV): "Therefore, confess your sins to one another and pray for one another, that you may be healed. The prayer of a righteous person has great power as it is working."

Addressing Concerns and Conflict Resolution

There are times when talking about fellow Christians becomes necessary to address concerns, correct wrongdoing, and promote reconciliation. In cases where there is a genuine need to address issues affecting individuals or the community, open and honest communication is crucial for restoration and growth.

Scriptural Support:

- Matthew 18:15 (ESV): "If your brother sins against you, go and tell him his fault, between you and him alone. If he listens to you, you have gained your brother."
- Galatians 6:1 (ESV): "Brothers, if anyone is caught in any transgression, you who are spiritual should restore him in a spirit of gentleness. Keep watch on yourself, lest you too be tempted."

Balancing Discretion and Love

While it can be appropriate to talk about fellow Christians, it is essential to balance discretion and love in our conversations. We should guard against gossip, slander, and idle talk that can harm reputations, spread discord, or violate confidentiality. Our words should be characterized by grace, truth, and a genuine desire to build up others.

Scriptural Support:

- Proverbs 11:13 (ASV): "He that goeth about as a tale-bearer revealeth secrets; But he that is of a faithful spirit concealeth a matter."
- 1 Peter 4:8 (ESV): "Above all, keep loving one another earnestly, since love covers a multitude of sins."

By understanding the context, purpose, and biblical principles related to talking about fellow Christians, we can engage in conversations that promote unity, edification, accountability, and reconciliation within the body of believers.

How may light talk turn into slander of the upright? What questions might we appropriately ask ourselves?

Light Talk Turning into Slander of the Upright

Light talk, which may initially seem harmless and casual, can gradually turn into slander of the upright if not carefully monitored and controlled. Slander involves making false or damaging statements about someone, tarnishing their reputation and causing harm. Light talk, if left unchecked, can evolve into malicious gossip and spreading untruths about others.

Scriptural Support:

- Proverbs 10:18 (ASV): "He that hideth hatred is of lying lips; And he that uttereth a slander is a fool."

- Proverbs 11:13 (ESV): "Whoever goes about slandering reveals secrets, but he who is trustworthy in spirit keeps a thing covered."

Appropriate Questions to Ask Ourselves

To prevent light talk from transforming into slander of the upright, it is important to ask ourselves thoughtful questions and evaluate our motives and actions. By examining our words and intentions, we can guard against engaging in harmful speech and promote a culture of love, respect, and edification.

Scriptural Support:

- Psalm 141:3 (ASV): "Set a watch, O Jehovah, before my mouth; Keep the door of my lips."

- Proverbs 16:23 (ESV): "The heart of the wise makes his speech judicious and adds persuasiveness to his lips."

Questions to Ask Ourselves:

1. **Is it true?** Before sharing information or engaging in conversation about others, we should ensure that what we say

is based on truth. Spreading false information can lead to slander and harm the reputation of the upright.

2. **Is it necessary?** We should consider the relevance and importance of the information we are sharing. Light talk that lacks purpose or significance can potentially escalate into gossip and slander.

3. **Is it kind and edifying?** Our words should be guided by kindness, love, and the desire to build up others. Engaging in conversations that uplift, encourage, and promote unity is far more beneficial than engaging in gossip or slander.

4. **Is it honoring God?** We should evaluate whether our words align with God's standards of truth, love, and integrity. Our speech should reflect the character of Christ and honor God in all that we say.

5. **Is it seeking resolution or reconciliation?** If there are concerns or conflicts with the upright, we should approach them in a spirit of gentleness and seek resolution or reconciliation. Engaging in slander or spreading rumors only perpetuates division and harm.

By regularly asking ourselves these questions and being mindful of our speech, we can prevent light talk from turning into slander of the upright. It is crucial to cultivate a heart that values truth, kindness, and building up others, reflecting the teachings and example of Jesus Christ.

According to Psalm 15:1, 3, what will we not do if we desire to be God's guest?

Qualifications to Be God's Guest

According to Psalm 15:1, 3, there are specific actions and behaviors that we must refrain from if we desire to be God's guest. These qualifications highlight the importance of righteous conduct and integrity in our relationship with God and others.

Scriptural Support:

- Psalm 15:1 (ASV): "O Jehovah, who shall sojourn in thy tabernacle? Who shall dwell in thy holy hill?"
- Psalm 15:3 (ESV): "who does not slander with his tongue and does no evil to his neighbor, nor takes up a reproach against his friend."

Refraining from Slander and Evil

To be God's guest, we must refrain from engaging in slander with our tongue and committing evil against our neighbor. Slander involves making false or damaging statements about others, tarnishing their reputation, and causing harm. Engaging in evil against our neighbor goes against God's command to love and treat others with kindness and respect.

Scriptural Support:

- Proverbs 10:18 (ESV): "The one who conceals hatred has lying lips, and whoever utters slander is a fool."
- Proverbs 14:21 (ASV): "He that despiseth his neighbor sinneth; But he that hath mercy on the poor, happy is he."

Avoiding Reproach and Gossip

Being God's guest also means avoiding taking up a reproach against our friend. This implies that we should not participate in gossip or speak negatively about others, even in private conversations. Instead, we are called to uphold the dignity and honor of our friends and associates.

Scriptural Support:

- Proverbs 17:9 (ESV): "Whoever covers an offense seeks love, but he who repeats a matter separates close friends."
- Proverbs 20:19 (ASV): "He that goeth about as a tale-bearer revealeth secrets; But he that is of a faithful spirit concealeth a matter."

By refraining from slander, evil, reproach, and gossip, we demonstrate a commitment to integrity, love, and respect in our interactions with others. These qualities are essential for those who desire to dwell in God's presence and be welcomed as His guests. It is through righteous conduct and upright speech that we honor God and cultivate healthy relationships with our neighbors and friends.

How may Acts 15:36-41 help us if we are tempted to gossip about one with whom we have a disagreement?

Lessons from Acts 15:36-41 for Resisting Gossip in Disagreements

Acts 15:36-41 provides valuable insights that can help us resist the temptation to gossip about someone with whom we have a disagreement. This passage highlights the importance of seeking reconciliation, maintaining unity, and extending grace and forgiveness towards others, even in times of conflict or disagreement.

Scriptural Support:

- Acts 15:36-41 (ESV): "And after some days Paul said to Barnabas, 'Let us return and visit the brothers in every city where we proclaimed the word of the Lord, and see how they are.' Now Barnabas wanted to take with them John called Mark. But Paul thought best not to take with them one who had withdrawn from them in Pamphylia and had not gone with them to the work. And there arose a sharp disagreement, so that they separated from each other. Barnabas took Mark with him and sailed away to Cyprus, but Paul chose Silas and departed, having been commended by the brothers to the grace of the Lord. And he went through Syria and Cilicia, strengthening the churches."

Seek Reconciliation and Restoration

Acts 15:36-41 reminds us of the importance of seeking reconciliation and restoration in relationships, rather than resorting to gossip or spreading negativity. Although Paul and Barnabas had a sharp disagreement regarding John Mark's involvement in their mission, they ultimately chose separate paths. However, this disagreement did not lead to public gossip or slander against one another. Instead, they remained focused on their respective ministries while still being committed to the work of the Lord.

Maintain Unity in the Body of Christ

The passage emphasizes the significance of maintaining unity within the body of Christ, even amidst disagreements. While Paul and Barnabas went their separate ways, they continued their respective ministries without engaging in malicious talk or undermining each other's work. Their actions demonstrate the importance of prioritizing the unity and effectiveness of the Church over personal disputes or disagreements.

Extend Grace and Forgiveness

Acts 15:36-41 teaches us the importance of extending grace and forgiveness, especially towards those with whom we have had disagreements. Although Paul and Barnabas disagreed about John Mark, there is no indication that they harbored resentment or held grudges against each other. They chose different companions for their journeys, yet they both continued to serve the Lord faithfully. This illustrates the need for grace, forgiveness, and the ability to move forward in unity and love.

Lessons for Resisting Gossip

From Acts 15:36-41, we can derive several lessons to help us resist the temptation to gossip about someone with whom we have a disagreement:

1. **Focus on the bigger mission:** Instead of dwelling on personal disagreements, maintain focus on the greater mission of serving God and furthering His kingdom.
2. **Respectfully address conflicts:** Seek to address conflicts and disagreements respectfully, with the goal of reconciliation and restoration.

3. **Avoid malicious talk:** Refrain from engaging in gossip, slander, or spreading negativity about others, even if there are disagreements.

4. **Prioritize unity and the welfare of the Church:** Recognize the importance of maintaining unity within the body of Christ, valuing the greater purpose of the Church above personal conflicts.

5. **Extend grace and forgiveness:** Show grace and forgiveness towards those with whom we have had disagreements, letting go of resentment and embracing a spirit of reconciliation.

By following these principles, we can resist the temptation to gossip and instead promote unity, reconciliation, and the welfare of the Church in times of disagreement or conflict.

As far as God's church is concerned, what can happen to an unrepentant slanderer? What caution must pastors exercise in connection with gossip and slander?

Consequences for Unrepentant Slanderers in God's Church

When it comes to God's church, unrepentant slanderers may face serious consequences. Slander is a grave sin that can cause significant harm to individuals and damage the unity and reputation of the church. God's Word provides insights into the consequences that an unrepentant slanderer may face within the context of the church community.

Scriptural Support:

- 1 Corinthians 5:11-13 (ESV): "But now I am writing to you not to associate with anyone who bears the name of brother if he is guilty of sexual immorality or greed, or is an idolater, reviler, drunkard, or swindler—not even to eat with such a one. For what have I to do with judging outsiders? Is it not those inside the church whom you are to judge? God judges those outside. 'Purge the evil person from among you.'"

- Titus 3:10-11 (ASV): "As for a man that is factious, after admonishing him once or twice, refuse to have anything to do with him; knowing that such a one is perverted, and sinneth, being self-condemned."

Caution for Pastors in Connection with Gossip and Slander

Pastors and church leaders have a crucial role in addressing gossip and slander within the church community. They must exercise caution and take appropriate measures to prevent the spread of gossip and to address slander when it occurs. This requires a commitment to upholding biblical principles, promoting a culture of love, and enforcing disciplinary actions when necessary.

Scriptural Support:

- James 3:1-2 (ESV): "Not many of you should become teachers, my brothers, for you know that we who teach will be judged with greater strictness. For we all stumble in many ways. And if anyone does not stumble in what he says, he is a perfect man, able also to bridle his whole body."
- 1 Timothy 5:19-20 (ESV): "Do not admit a charge against an elder except on the evidence of two or three witnesses. As for those who persist in sin, rebuke them in the presence of all, so that the rest may stand in fear."

Exercise Caution:

1. **Address the issue promptly:** Pastors should address gossip and slander promptly and address the individuals involved in a loving, yet firm manner, encouraging repentance and reconciliation.
2. **Promote biblical teaching:** Pastors have a responsibility to teach and emphasize the biblical principles of love, forgiveness, and the building up of one another. By promoting a culture of edifying speech, pastors can help prevent gossip and slander from taking root.

3. **Enforce church discipline:** In cases where gossip and slander persist and individuals remain unrepentant, pastors may need to implement church discipline as prescribed in Scripture. This may include exclusion from certain privileges or, in severe cases, temporary or permanent removal from the church community.

4. **Provide pastoral care:** In dealing with gossip and slander, pastors should also provide pastoral care, offering guidance, support, and opportunities for repentance and restoration for those involved.

By exercising caution and following biblical principles, pastors can effectively address gossip and slander, protect the unity and integrity of the church, and promote an environment of love, forgiveness, and growth within the body of Christ.

Instead of gossiping about a wrongdoer, what should you do?

Response to a Wrongdoer Instead of Gossiping

Instead of gossiping about a wrongdoer, the Bible provides guidance on how we should respond in such situations. Rather than engaging in gossip, our approach should be characterized by love, humility, and a desire for restoration and reconciliation.

Scriptural Support:

- Matthew 18:15 (ESV): "If your brother sins against you, go and tell him his fault, between you and him alone. If he listens to you, you have gained your brother."

- Galatians 6:1 (ASV): "Brethren, even if a man be overtaken in any trespass, ye who are spiritual, restore such a one in a spirit of gentleness; looking to thyself, lest thou also be tempted."

Approach the Individual Privately

When confronted with the wrongdoing of another person, the Bible encourages us to address the issue directly with the individual involved. Instead of spreading gossip or discussing the matter with others, we are instructed to approach the wrongdoer privately, seeking to resolve the matter in a one-on-one conversation. This approach allows for open communication and the possibility of resolution without unnecessarily involving others.

Seek Restoration and Reconciliation

In dealing with a wrongdoer, our goal should be restoration and reconciliation rather than gossip or condemnation. We are called to approach the individual in a spirit of gentleness and love, seeking to help them recognize their error and encouraging them to turn away from it. The focus is on restoring the relationship and guiding the wrongdoer towards repentance and growth.

Exercise Humility and Self-Reflection

As we address the wrongdoing of others, it is important to exercise humility and self-reflection. We should be mindful of our own weaknesses and vulnerabilities, recognizing that we too are capable of falling into sin. This mindset helps us approach the situation with grace and understanding, rather than a judgmental or condemning attitude.

Encourage Personal Growth and Accountability

In addition to addressing the wrongdoing with the individual, we can encourage personal growth and accountability. This may involve offering support, guidance, and prayer, as well as holding the wrongdoer accountable for their actions in a loving and respectful manner. The ultimate aim is to help the person grow spiritually and avoid further transgressions.

By following these biblical principles, we can respond to a wrongdoer in a manner that promotes healing, restoration, and reconciliation, rather than engaging in gossip or spreading negativity. Our focus should be on lovingly addressing the issue and seeking the well-being and spiritual growth of both the wrongdoer and the affected relationships.

Why can we say that 1 Corinthians 1:11 does not authorize gossiping?

1 Corinthians 1:11 and the Absence of Authorization for Gossiping

1 Corinthians 1:11 does not provide authorization for gossiping. The verse addresses a specific issue within the Corinthian church, highlighting the presence of divisions and quarrels among the believers. However, the passage does not condone or promote gossip as a solution or appropriate response to these conflicts. Instead, it emphasizes the importance of unity and harmony within the body of Christ.

Scriptural Support:

- 1 Corinthians 1:11 (ESV): "For it has been reported to me by Chloe's people that there is quarreling among you, my brothers."

Identification of a Problem

1 Corinthians 1:11 highlights the existence of quarreling and divisions within the Corinthian church. Chloe's people had reported this issue to the apostle Paul, drawing attention to the internal conflicts that were undermining the unity and witness of the believers.

Emphasis on Unity and Harmony

While the verse acknowledges the problem of quarreling, it does not authorize or encourage gossip as a means to address or perpetuate these conflicts. Rather, the broader context of the letter emphasizes the importance of unity, humility, and love within the body of Christ.

Scriptural Support:

- 1 Corinthians 1:10 (ESV): "I appeal to you, brothers, by the name of our Lord Jesus Christ, that all of you agree, and that there be no divisions among you, but that you be united in the same mind and the same judgment."

- 1 Corinthians 3:3 (ASV): "for ye are yet carnal: for whereas there is among you jealousy and strife, are ye not carnal, and do ye not walk after the manner of men?"

Resolution through Godly Wisdom

Rather than endorsing gossip or perpetuating divisions, the Apostle Paul provides guidance on resolving conflicts in a godly manner. Throughout the letter, he emphasizes the need for wisdom, love, and reconciliation as the means to address disputes and promote unity within the church.

Scriptural Support:

- 1 Corinthians 3:16 (ESV): "Do you not know that you are God's temple and that God's Spirit dwells in you?"
- 1 Corinthians 6:7 (ASV): "Nay, already it is altogether a defect in you, that ye have lawsuits one with another. Why not rather take wrong? why not rather be defrauded?"
- 1 Corinthians 13:4-7 (ESV): "Love is patient and kind; love does not envy or boast; it is not arrogant or rude. It does not insist on its own way; it is not irritable or resentful; it does not rejoice at wrongdoing, but rejoices with the truth. Love bears all things, believes all things, hopes all things, endures all things."

In summary, while 1 Corinthians 1:11 acknowledges the presence of quarreling within the Corinthian church, it does not authorize or encourage gossiping as a solution. Instead, the broader context of the letter emphasizes the importance of unity, love, and godly wisdom in resolving conflicts and fostering a harmonious environment within the body of Christ.

Helping someone overcome gossiping requires a tailored approach, as the motivations and implications of this behavior may vary greatly from person to person. Here are some questions that can initiate a meaningful conversation and facilitate change:

TURN OLD HABITS INTO NEW HABITS

1. **What makes a piece of information about someone else interesting to you?** This can help the person understand what draws them to gossip in the first place.

2. **How do you feel when you engage in gossiping?** Understanding the emotional payoff, such as feeling included or superior, can be a first step towards change.

3. **Have you considered the potential harm that gossiping might cause to others and to your relationships?** Acknowledging the potential damage can instigate a change in behavior.

4. **How would you feel if someone were gossiping about you?** Encouraging empathy can help the person see the issue from another perspective.

5. **Do you use gossip to fit in or feel part of a group?** This can highlight whether gossip is a social tool for the person.

6. **Are there topics or types of information that you feel should be off-limits for gossiping?** Establishing boundaries can be a good starting point to reducing gossip.

7. **Do you find it difficult to stop gossiping once you've started?** This can help identify if they need help with impulse control or finding other topics of conversation.

8. **What positive interactions could replace gossip in your conversations?** Identifying other ways to connect can help reduce reliance on gossip.

9. **Are you ready and willing to make changes to your behavior?** Their commitment to change is crucial.

10. **Would you consider seeking help from a counselor or therapist to understand your tendency to gossip and develop strategies to overcome it?** If gossiping is deeply ingrained, they might benefit from professional help.

Remember, these questions should be asked in a non-judgmental, empathetic way. Change takes time and requires understanding, self-reflection, and often, professional support.

Christian Counseling and Biblical Principles

Embodying the Principle of Love in Speech

The Apostle Paul writes in Ephesians 4:15 (ESV) that we should speak "the truth in love," which highlights two significant factors in overcoming gossip. The Greek word used for love in this verse is "agape," denoting a selfless, sacrificial love that seeks the best for others. Embodying this kind of love will naturally steer us away from engaging in harmful gossip.

Proverbs 17:9 (ASV) further supports this, stating, "He that covereth a transgression seeketh love; But he that harpeth on a matter separateth chief friends." It suggests that love often involves choosing not to expose the failings of others unnecessarily. If our words aren't motivated by and filled with love (agape), it's best to hold them back.

Exercising Wisdom in Speech

The book of Proverbs repeatedly emphasizes the value of wisdom, including in our speech. Proverbs 10:19 (ASV) observes, "In the multitude of words there wanteth not transgression; But he that refraineth his lips doeth wisely." The Hebrew word for wisdom, "chokmah," involves a practical, moral understanding that shapes our actions—including our words. The wisdom expressed here is the discernment to speak less and listen more, reducing the opportunities for gossip.

Guarding the Tongue

James 3:5 (ESV) warns, "So also the tongue is a small member, yet it boasts of great things. How great a forest is set ablaze by such a small fire!" The Greek word for "set ablaze," "phlogizō," provides a potent image of the damage gossip can cause, likening it to a wildfire that destroys everything in its path. James encourages Christians to exercise control over their tongues, a reminder that is particularly relevant for those struggling with gossip.

Cognitive Behavioral Therapy (CBT) Approach

Identifying and Challenging Cognitive Distortions

CBT aims to identify and challenge cognitive distortions—unhealthy patterns of thinking that can lead to destructive behaviors, such as gossiping. One common cognitive distortion is "labeling," where a person assigns negative labels to themselves or others. By identifying and challenging this and other distortions, individuals can begin to change the thought patterns that drive their gossiping.

Developing Empathy

CBT also promotes the development of empathy—understanding and sharing the feelings of others. This is often achieved through exercises like perspective-taking, where individuals are encouraged to imagine how others might feel if they were the subject of gossip.

Using Mindfulness Techniques

Mindfulness techniques can also be effective in managing gossip. By cultivating an increased awareness of their thoughts, feelings, and behaviors, individuals can recognize the urge to gossip when it arises and choose a more positive course of action. Mindfulness can also help individuals stay focused on the present, reducing the temptation to discuss past events or speculate about the future—common elements in gossip.

Building Effective Communication Skills

CBT typically includes training in effective communication skills. This can help individuals express their thoughts and feelings in a direct, assertive way, reducing the need to engage in indirect, harmful communication like gossip. Techniques might include using "I" statements, expressing needs clearly, and practicing active listening.

In conclusion, both Christian counseling and CBT offer valuable insights and practical strategies for overcoming gossip. By integrating these approaches, individuals can begin to experience transformation, renewal of their minds (ἀνακαίνωσις, anakainōsis)—in this crucial area of their lives. It's not a quick fix but a journey of growth and change, requiring commitment, practice, and God's grace.

CHAPTER 17 How Do You Get Control Over Being Consistently Late?

Questions and Answers

Helping someone overcome consistent lateness involves exploring the reasons behind their behavior and offering solutions. Here are some specific questions that can be asked:

1. **Are you aware that you're often late?** Some people don't realize they have an issue with punctuality.

2. **How do you manage your time?** This will help identify if the person lacks time management skills.

3. **Do you often underestimate how long tasks will take?** Many chronically late individuals misjudge the amount of time needed for tasks.

4. **What's typically happening when you realize you're going to be late?** Understanding what is happening when they're running late can offer insights into patterns and potential solutions.

5. **What consequences have you faced due to your lateness?** The impacts of their tardiness on their work, relationships, and personal life might motivate them to change.

6. **Do you believe being late communicates disrespect for other people's time?** This question can help them understand the implications of their lateness from a different perspective.

7. **Are there specific situations where you're more likely to be late than others?** This can help to identify patterns and particular scenarios that cause trouble.

8. **What steps have you previously taken to try and improve your punctuality?** Their past attempts at resolution can indicate what methods might work for them in the future.

9. **Are you willing to commit to improving your time management?** This question assesses their readiness and commitment to make a change.

10. **Would you consider seeking help from a coach or professional specializing in time management?** They might benefit from professional guidance if lateness is seriously affecting their life.

It's crucial to ask these questions in a supportive and understanding manner. Keep in mind that overcoming consistent lateness often involves changing established habits, which takes time and commitment.

Biblical Stewardship of Time

Our time is a gift from God, and how we use it demonstrates our respect for Him and His creation. Ephesians 5:15-16 (ESV) instructs us to "Look carefully then how you walk, not as unwise but as wise, making the best use of the time, because the days are evil." The Greek word used for "making the best use" is "exagorazó," which implies redeeming, acquiring, or making wise and purposeful use of something. This suggests we should be conscientious about our time management, including our promptness.

Respecting Others Through Punctuality

Being consistently late often impacts other people, not just us. Paul writes in Philippians 2:3-4 (ESV): "Do nothing from selfish ambition or conceit, but in humility count others more significant than yourselves. Let each of you look not only to his own interests, but also to the interests of others." Our punctuality, or lack thereof, can demonstrate our consideration for others and their time.

Practicing Diligence and Discipline

Proverbs 21:5 (ASV) states, "The plans of the diligent lead surely to plenty, But those of everyone who is hasty, surely to poverty." The Hebrew term for "diligent" in this verse is "charuwts," signifying determination and strenuous effort. One aspect of diligence is discipline, including the discipline to be punctual.

Cognitive Behavioral Therapy (CBT) Approach

Understanding the Impact of Being Late

The first step in CBT would be to help the individual understand the effects of their consistent lateness, both on themselves and others. This can provide motivation for change.

Identifying Underlying Beliefs and Thoughts

CBT would seek to identify any underlying beliefs or thoughts contributing to the habitual lateness. For example, the individual might believe that their time is more valuable than others, leading them to de-prioritize punctuality.

Developing Time Management Skills

CBT would likely include practical strategies for improving time management skills. This might involve learning to estimate time more accurately, schedule tasks more effectively, or avoid procrastination.

Implementing Behavioral Changes

CBT involves setting specific, measurable, achievable, relevant, and time-bound (SMART) goals. In this case, the individual might set a goal to arrive on time for all appointments in the next week. The therapist would help them develop a plan for achieving this goal and monitor their progress.

Using Cognitive Restructuring Techniques

Cognitive restructuring can help the individual change unhelpful thoughts or beliefs that contribute to their lateness. For example, they might learn to challenge the thought "It doesn't matter if I'm a few minutes late" with a more helpful thought like "Being on time shows respect for others."

With the combined power of Biblical principles and Cognitive Behavioral Therapy tools, the challenge of consistent lateness can be overcome. As with the transformation mentioned in Romans 12:2, it involves the 'anakainōsis'—the making new or renewal—of one's mind, driving changes in thought patterns and behaviors, bringing them closer to God's standards. Remember, God is not just the God of second chances; He is the God of new beginnings. Embrace His grace, and let it drive you towards punctuality, respect for others, and wise stewardship of the time He has given you.

CHAPTER 18 How Do You Get Control of Overspending or Not Budgeting Properly?

Questions and Answers

Helping someone to overcome overspending or improper budgeting involves understanding their financial habits, attitudes, and goals. Here are some specific questions to guide your conversation:

1. **What is your understanding of your current financial situation?** This can help you gauge their awareness of their finances.
2. **Do you have a budget? If not, why? If yes, what difficulties do you encounter when trying to stick to it?** Understanding their existing relationship with budgeting can offer insights into potential obstacles and solutions.
3. **What leads you to spend more than you've budgeted or can afford?** Identifying triggers for overspending can help create strategies to combat them.
4. **Do you frequently make impulse purchases?** This question can help uncover if lack of impulse control is a contributing factor.
5. **What emotions do you often associate with spending?** Emotional spending can be a significant factor in overspending.
6. **Do you understand the long-term impacts of overspending and debt on your financial health?** This can highlight if they're aware of the risks and consequences of their financial behaviors.
7. **How confident are you in your financial knowledge and skills?** A lack of financial literacy can be a big factor in overspending and not budgeting properly.

8. **What are your financial goals, both short-term and long-term?** Clearly defined goals can motivate changes in financial behaviors.
9. **Are you willing to make changes to your spending and budgeting habits?** Their readiness and commitment to change are key in this process.
10. **Would you consider seeking help from a financial advisor or taking a financial literacy course?** If overspending is a chronic issue, they might benefit from professional assistance or further education.

Remember, these questions should be asked in a supportive, non-judgmental way. Changing financial behaviors often requires a mindset shift, new skills, and time.

Biblical Stewardship and Responsibility

Managing our finances wisely is part of our stewardship responsibilities. Proverbs 27:23-24 (ASV) advises, "Be thou diligent to know the state of thy flocks, and look well to thy herds: For riches are not forever..." This proverb, though referring to agricultural assets, underlines the importance of being knowledgeable and proactive about one's resources, which applies to our personal finances as well.

The Wisdom of Planning and Budgeting

Planning ahead is highlighted in the Bible. In the Parable of the Wise and Foolish Builders in Luke 14:28-30 (ESV), Jesus taught the importance of counting the cost before building a tower. This principle is directly applicable to our personal finances—we should plan and budget to ensure we can 'complete our tower,' i.e., meet our financial obligations and goals.

Avoiding the Trap of Materialism

1 Timothy 6:9-10 (ESV) warns about the love of money leading to all sorts of evil. The Greek word for 'love of money' is "philarguria,"

which signifies an unhealthy affection for wealth. This passage warns us against materialism and emphasizes the need for contentment.

Cognitive Behavioral Therapy (CBT) Approach

Understanding the Impact of Overspending

CBT would first help individuals realize the impacts of overspending on their lives. This includes financial stress, debt, and potential conflict with family members or significant others.

Identifying Underlying Beliefs and Thoughts

CBT would explore any underlying beliefs or thoughts that contribute to overspending. These might include beliefs like 'I deserve to treat myself,' or 'Having the latest products makes me more valuable.'

Developing Budgeting Skills

CBT can offer practical strategies for improving budgeting skills. This might involve learning to track expenses, setting spending limits, and planning for future needs and wants.

Implementing Behavioral Changes

Just as in the previous section, CBT involves setting SMART goals. Here, the individual might set a goal to stay within a certain budget for the next month. The therapist would help them develop a plan for achieving this goal and monitor their progress.

Cognitive Restructuring Techniques

These techniques can help change unhelpful thoughts or beliefs that lead to overspending. They might learn to challenge thoughts like 'I can't resist a sale,' with more helpful thoughts like 'I can choose to only buy what I need and have budgeted for.'

Applying these principles and strategies can help transform a habit of overspending into wise stewardship. The 'anakainōsis'—the renovation of the mind—that Romans 12:2 talks about, implies that change and renewal are a continuous process. As we strive to align our lives more closely with God's standards, we can rely on His grace and strength to help us overcome our struggles. He makes all things new, and that includes our attitudes and behaviors around money and possessions.

CHAPTER 19 How Do You Get Control Over Being a Chronic Complainer?

Questions and Answers

Overcoming chronic complaining necessitates an understanding of the reasons and rewards behind the behavior. Here are some questions to guide the conversation:

1. **Do you feel that you complain often?** Sometimes people are not aware of their habitual complaining.

2. **What usually triggers your complaints?** This can help identify patterns in their complaining behavior.

3. **How do you feel when you complain?** This question can reveal the emotional payoffs of their behavior.

4. **How do you think your complaints affect those around you?** Chronic complaining can negatively impact relationships and this understanding might motivate change.

5. **Have you received feedback about your complaining from others?** It's valuable to understand how others perceive their behavior.

6. **Do you feel your complaints are usually justified?** This can provide insight into their perception of fairness and expectations from life.

7. **Have you tried to limit your complaining in the past?** This can inform what strategies they have tried and how successful these were.

8. **Could there be alternative ways to express your dissatisfaction?** Identifying alternative, constructive ways to voice concerns is crucial.

9. **Are you ready to make changes to reduce your complaining?** Their willingness to change is essential for progress.

10. **Would you consider seeking professional help, such as a coach or therapist, to work on this issue?** Chronic complaining can sometimes indicate deeper issues that may require professional help.

These questions should be approached with empathy and understanding. Remember, changing habitual behaviors requires time, commitment, and often professional support.

Biblical Perspective on Complaining

The Bible is clear about the harmful nature of complaining. Philippians 2:14-15 (ESV) instructs, "Do everything without grumbling or arguing, so that you may become blameless and pure..." The Greek word for 'grumbling' used here is "goggusmos," which refers to the expression of discontent or complaint, generally secret or not openly avowed.

God's Response to Complaining

God's response to complaining is illustrated vividly in the story of the Israelites in the wilderness in Numbers 11:1 (ASV), "And the people complained in the hearing of the Lord about their misfortunes, and when the Lord heard it, his anger was kindled..."

Fostering a Heart of Gratitude

The antidote to chronic complaining is cultivating a heart of gratitude. 1 Thessalonians 5:18 (ESV) reminds us, "Give thanks in all circumstances; for this is the will of God in Christ Jesus for you." The Greek word for 'give thanks' is "eucharisteo," meaning to express gratitude, to show oneself as grateful - often with the implication of an accompanying feeling of thankfulness.

The Power of the Tongue

Proverbs 18:21 (ASV) underscores, "Death and life are in the power of the tongue..." Understanding the weight of our words can motivate us to replace our complaints with praise and thanksgiving.

Cognitive Behavioral Therapy (CBT) Perspective and Tools

Awareness and Understanding

CBT first requires awareness and understanding of the problem behavior, in this case, chronic complaining. This involves identifying when and why complaining happens.

Challenging Irrational Beliefs

CBT would then help the person challenge any irrational beliefs related to their complaining, such as the notion that complaining gets them what they want, or that it's a way to connect with others.

Cognitive Restructuring

Cognitive restructuring involves changing thought patterns that lead to unwanted behaviors. The individual would learn to reframe negative thoughts and situations, moving from complaints to gratitude or problem-solving.

Developing and Implementing Coping Strategies

CBT would assist the individual in developing coping strategies for times when the urge to complain arises. This could involve mindfulness techniques, stress management strategies, or finding healthier ways to express dissatisfaction.

Accountability and Reinforcement

CBT encourages ongoing accountability and reinforcement of new behaviors. This could be through regular follow-up with a therapist or accountability with a trusted friend or family member.

In conclusion, Romans 12:2's call for a "renewal of your mind" applies profoundly in overcoming chronic complaining. This renewing—anakainōsis in the original Greek—does not refer to a one-time change but a continuous transformation process. Through the interplay of biblical wisdom and CBT tools, one can turn the habit of chronic complaining into a lifestyle marked by gratitude and positivity. As believers striving to reflect Christ, this change benefits not just ourselves but also those around us, painting a more accurate picture of the hope and joy found in our faith.

CHAPTER 20 How Do You Get Control Over Not Listening Actively to Others?

Questions and Answers

Addressing the issue of not actively listening to others requires probing into the person's communication style, their perceptions of conversations, and their awareness of the issue. Here are some specific questions to ask:

1. **Are you aware that you may not be actively listening during conversations?** Sometimes people are unaware of their poor listening habits.

2. **What usually happens when you find yourself not actively listening?** This can help identify distractions or situations that trigger their lack of active listening.

3. **Do you often find your mind wandering during conversations?** This can point to attention issues that may need to be addressed.

4. **How do you respond when someone is speaking to you?** Their answer can reveal whether they are typically formulating responses or thinking about something else instead of focusing on what the speaker is saying.

5. **Have you ever received feedback about your listening skills?** Understanding how others perceive their listening can motivate them to change.

6. **Do you feel you understand and remember what others say to you?** This can provide insights into their perception of their listening skills.

7. **What techniques have you tried to improve your listening skills, if any?** Learning about their past attempts can inform which methods might work for them in the future.

8. **Are you willing to work on improving your active listening skills?** Their readiness and commitment to change are key factors in the process.

9. **Do you often feel rushed or impatient during conversations?** This can help to identify if they need help managing stress or developing patience.

10. **Would you consider seeking help from a coach or therapist to improve your active listening skills?** If the lack of active listening is significantly affecting their relationships or work, they might benefit from professional guidance.

Remember, these questions should be asked in a supportive, non-judgmental way. Improving listening skills often involves changing entrenched habits, which requires time, patience, and often professional support.

The Biblical Imperative of Active Listening

One key biblical principle underlying active listening is found in James 1:19 (ESV), "Know this, my beloved brothers: let every person be quick to hear, slow to speak, slow to anger." The Greek word "tachys" translates to "quick" and carries the connotation of readiness or eagerness. It suggests that we should be ready and eager to listen - to be active participants in the process of hearing and understanding others.

The Model of Jesus Christ

Jesus Christ provides the ultimate model of active listening. Throughout the Gospels, we see Jesus fully engaged with those around Him. He asked probing questions and genuinely cared about people's responses. In John 4, Jesus' interaction with the Samaritan woman demonstrates His ability to listen and understand deeply, crossing cultural and societal barriers to bring truth and healing.

The Virtue of Humility in Listening

Proverbs 12:15 (ASV) advises, "The way of a fool is right in his own eyes: But he that is wise hearkeneth unto counsel." To be an active listener, we must practice humility, acknowledging that we have much to learn from others. The Hebrew word "shama," translated as "hearkeneth" here, involves not only hearing but also understanding and responding to what is being said.

Understanding Others Through Empathy

Romans 12:15 (ESV) encourages us to "Rejoice with those who rejoice, weep with those who weep." The Greek word "sygchairo" and "sympatheo," translated as 'rejoice with' and 'weep with,' respectively, carry the notion of being so closely identified with others that we share their joy and their sorrow.

Cognitive Behavioral Therapy (CBT) Approach to Active Listening

Cognitive Awareness and Restructuring

In CBT, understanding the cognitive processes behind not listening actively is the first step towards change. Individuals must learn to identify the cognitive distortions (like overgeneralization, jumping to conclusions, mind reading) that prevent them from listening effectively and learn to restructure these thoughts.

Mindfulness Training

Mindfulness training, a key component of many CBT approaches, can also be beneficial for improving active listening. Mindfulness involves focusing one's full attention on the present moment, which can help individuals stay engaged during conversations and avoid distractions.

Communication Skills Training

CBT also includes direct training in communication skills. This could involve learning and practicing techniques like summarizing what the other person said, asking clarifying questions, and providing feedback, all of which are components of active listening.

Behavioral Activation and Practice

Behavioral activation is another important aspect of CBT. Once individuals have learned new listening skills, they must practice these skills in real-life settings. This could involve setting specific goals for using active listening techniques in conversations and then reviewing these experiences in therapy to identify successes and areas for improvement.

In essence, we can see a profound interplay between the principles of active listening as espoused in the Bible and those in CBT. The process of renewal, or "anakainōsis," of our minds, as mentioned in Romans 12:2, goes hand in hand with the cognitive restructuring processes in CBT. As we commit to this journey, we transform our old habits into new ones, becoming not only better listeners but also better followers of Christ.

CHAPTER 21 How Do You Get Control Over Holding Grudges?

Questions and Answers

Helping someone overcome holding grudges requires understanding the root of their resentment and their readiness to let go. Here are some specific questions to guide your conversation:

1. **Do you often find yourself holding onto grudges?** This can help the individual recognize their habitual resentment.

2. **What usually triggers you to hold a grudge?** Understanding their triggers can help identify patterns and potential solutions.

3. **How does holding a grudge make you feel?** This can help them understand the emotional payoff or cost of their behavior.

4. **How do these grudges affect your relationships and your well-being?** This can highlight the negative impacts of their behavior, which may motivate change.

5. **Do you believe holding a grudge serves you in any way?** Some people believe their grudges protect them in some way; this question can help explore that belief.

6. **Have you tried to let go of your grudges in the past? If so, what difficulties did you encounter?** Understanding past attempts can provide insights into what strategies might or might not work.

7. **How might your life be different if you didn't hold grudges?** Imagining a grudge-free life might help them see the benefits of change.

8. **Are you ready to start working on letting go of grudges?** Their willingness to change is crucial for progress.

9. **What steps could you take to forgive and move on from a past hurt?** This can help them start thinking about practical steps towards forgiveness.

10. **Would you consider seeking help from a counselor or therapist to learn strategies for letting go of grudges?** If grudge-holding is deeply ingrained, they might benefit from professional help.

Remember, these questions should be asked in a supportive and understanding way. Letting go of grudges often involves dealing with past hurts and requires time, emotional work, and often professional support.

The Biblical Perspective on Holding Grudges

Holding grudges is a form of resentment and unforgiveness that can deeply affect one's spiritual health. Ephesians 4:31-32 (ESV) admonishes, "Let all bitterness and wrath and anger and clamor and slander be put away from you, along with all malice. Be kind to one another, tenderhearted, forgiving one another, as God in Christ forgave you." The Greek term "pikria," translated as bitterness, carries connotations of deep-seated grudges. We are not merely advised, but instructed to rid ourselves of such emotions.

The Role of Forgiveness

Matthew 18:21-22 (ESV) provides a clear directive on forgiveness, "Then Peter came up and said to him, 'Lord, how often will my brother sin against me, and I forgive him? As many as seven times?' Jesus said to him, 'I do not say to you seven times, but seventy-seven times.'" Jesus' hyperbolic response emphasizes the limitless nature of forgiveness. In the Greek text, "seventy-seven times" can also be interpreted as "seventy times seven," further emphasizing its unlimitedness.

The Path to Reconciliation

In Matthew 5:23-24 (ESV), Jesus instructs, "So if you are offering your gift at the altar and there remember that your brother has something against you, leave your gift there before the altar and go. First be reconciled to your brother, and then come and offer your gift." The Greek term "diallage," translated here as reconcile, implies a change from enmity to friendship. It is a call to resolve our conflicts and let go of our grudges.

Practicing Love Over Hate

Leviticus 19:18 (ASV) states, "Thou shalt not take vengeance, nor bear any grudge against the children of thy people, but thou shalt love thy neighbor as thyself: I am the LORD." The Hebrew term "naqam," translated here as vengeance, along with "nasa," translated as bear grudge, warn us against harboring ill feelings. We are instead called to love (Hebrew: "ahab") our neighbors as ourselves.

Cognitive Behavioral Therapy (CBT) Approach to Releasing Grudges

Cognitive Techniques: Challenging Negative Thoughts

In CBT, holding grudges is often viewed as a cognitive distortion, particularly "personalization," where a person internalizes and personalizes events with negative interpretations. CBT techniques such as cognitive restructuring help individuals challenge and change these distorted thoughts.

Behavioral Techniques: Forgiveness Interventions

CBT practitioners may employ forgiveness interventions that encourage the person to replace negative thoughts about the offender with more positive or neutral ones. This is consistent with the Biblical principle of forgiving as God in Christ forgave us.

Mindfulness and Acceptance

Mindfulness-based CBT techniques can also be valuable in addressing grudges. Through mindfulness, individuals learn to recognize and accept their feelings without judgment, allowing them to let go of resentment and unforgiveness.

Emotion Regulation Strategies

Emotion regulation is another critical component of CBT that can help with grudge-holding. By learning and practicing skills to manage intense emotions, individuals can prevent resentment from escalating into grudges.

Practicing Empathy

Practicing empathy is also vital, both in the Biblical context and in CBT. By understanding the perspectives and experiences of others, it becomes easier to forgive and let go of grudges.

Overall, the Biblical principle of "anakainōsis," or the renewal of our minds, works harmoniously with CBT's aim to challenge and change maladaptive thought processes. As we continually renew our minds in accordance with Biblical teachings and apply CBT's practical strategies, we can overcome the habit of holding grudges and achieve healthier, more fulfilling relationships.

CHAPTER 22 How Do You Get Control Over Your Pornography Addiction?

Questions and Answers

How does pornography affect individuals?

The Effects of Pornography on Individuals

Pornography has profound effects on individuals, impacting them emotionally, mentally, relationally, and spiritually. Here are some key areas where individuals may be affected by pornography:

1. Distorted View of Sexuality Exposure to pornography can distort one's view of human sexuality, presenting a skewed and unrealistic representation of intimate relationships. It objectifies individuals, promotes harmful stereotypes, and may create unrealistic expectations about physical appearance, performance, and sexual relationships.

2. Emotional and Psychological Consequences Engaging in pornography can lead to a range of negative emotional and psychological consequences. Feelings of guilt, shame, and diminished self-worth are common. It may contribute to anxiety, depression, and difficulties in forming healthy relationships. Proverbs 6:25 (ESV) warns, "Do not desire her beauty in your heart, and do not let her capture you with her eyelashes."

3. Relationship Strain Pornography can negatively impact relationships, causing strain, mistrust, and communication breakdown. It can create unrealistic expectations, erode intimacy, and lead to feelings of betrayal. Matthew 5:28 (ESV) highlights the importance of guarding one's thoughts and desires, stating, "But I say to you that everyone who looks at a woman with lustful intent has already committed adultery with her in his heart."

4. Spiritual Consequences From a spiritual perspective, pornography consumption can lead to spiritual bondage, distancing individuals from God and His intended plan for their lives. It can hinder spiritual growth, compromise one's integrity, and erode the sense of holiness. Galatians 5:19-21 (ASV) warns against engaging in sinful behaviors, including sexual immorality, stating, "Now the works of the flesh are evident: sexual immorality, impurity, sensuality... those who do such things will not inherit the kingdom of God."

5. Addiction and Escalation Pornography has the potential to become addictive, leading to a cycle of compulsive behavior and a need for increasing levels of explicit content to achieve the same level of stimulation. This addiction can disrupt daily life, impair functioning, and lead to a loss of control over one's behaviors.

6. Impact on Physical Health While the primary impact of pornography is on the emotional, mental, and spiritual well-being, excessive pornography use may also have physical consequences. It can contribute to sexual dysfunction, decrease sexual satisfaction, and impair overall sexual health.

Seeking Healing and Restoration Recognizing the damaging effects of pornography is the first step towards seeking healing and restoration. Through self-reflection, accountability, counseling, and relying on God's grace, individuals can find hope and recovery. It is important to cultivate a renewed mind and fill it with wholesome thoughts and pursuits. Romans 12:2 (ESV) encourages believers to be transformed by the renewal of their minds, stating, "Do not be conformed to this world, but be transformed by the renewal of your mind."

By seeking support from trustworthy individuals, engaging in healthy relationships, pursuing therapy, and seeking spiritual guidance, individuals can overcome the harmful effects of pornography and experience healing, restoration, and a renewed understanding of healthy sexuality according to God's design.

According to Proverbs 9:13-18, to what does one of the invitations lead? (Prov. 2:11-19; 5:3-10) What choice is presented?

The Invitation and its Consequences

According to Proverbs 9:13-18, one of the invitations leads to destruction and death. This passage presents a contrast between two invitations: the invitation of Wisdom and the invitation of Folly. Let's explore the Scriptures that shed light on these invitations and the choices presented.

1. The Invitation of Wisdom Proverbs 9:10-12 (ESV) states: "The fear of the LORD is the beginning of wisdom, and the knowledge of the Holy One is insight. For by me your days will be multiplied, and years will be added to your life. If you are wise, you are wise for yourself; if you scoff, you alone will bear it."

This passage emphasizes the importance of the fear of the Lord and the pursuit of wisdom. The invitation of Wisdom leads to understanding, long life, and blessings. It encourages individuals to seek godly wisdom and make choices that align with God's principles.

2. The Invitation of Folly Proverbs 9:13-18 (ESV) describes the invitation of Folly: "The woman Folly is loud; she is seductive and knows nothing. She sits at the door of her house; she takes a seat on the highest places of the town, calling to those who pass by, who are going straight on their way, 'Whoever is simple, let him turn in here!' And to him who lacks sense she says, 'Stolen water is sweet, and bread eaten in secret is pleasant.' But he does not know that the dead are there, that her guests are in the depths of Sheol."

This passage portrays Folly as a seductive and deceptive figure who entices those lacking wisdom and understanding. The invitation of Folly may appear appealing and alluring, promising pleasure and excitement. However, its ultimate outcome is destruction and death.

The Choice and its Consequences The passage in Proverbs presents individuals with a choice between two paths: the path of

Wisdom or the path of Folly. It highlights the importance of discernment and making wise decisions based on godly principles. The consequences of choosing the invitation of Folly include spiritual and moral ruin, brokenness, and separation from God's blessings.

Proverbs 2:11-19 (ASV) and Proverbs 5:3-10 (ESV) further warn about the consequences of yielding to the invitation of Folly. These passages caution against falling into the trap of immorality, adultery, and destructive behaviors that can bring ruin to one's life and relationships.

In summary, Proverbs 9:13-18 portrays the contrasting invitations of Wisdom and Folly. While the invitation of Wisdom leads to blessings and life, the invitation of Folly leads to destruction and death. It emphasizes the importance of choosing wisdom, discernment, and godly principles in order to walk in the paths of righteousness and experience the abundant life that God intends for His people.

What are some reasons why we should avoid sexually immoral conduct? (Prov. 5:15-18; 1 Cor. 6:9, 10; Prov. 7:23, 26; 9:13-18)

Reasons to Avoid Sexually Immoral Conduct

1. **Preservation of Marriage and Intimacy**: Proverbs 5:15-18 (ASV) emphasizes the importance of marital fidelity and sexual satisfaction within the context of marriage. It encourages individuals to find joy and fulfillment in their own spouse, promoting a committed and exclusive relationship.

2. **Consequences of Immorality**: 1 Corinthians 6:9-10 (ESV) warns about the consequences of engaging in sexually immoral conduct. It states that those who practice such behaviors will not inherit the kingdom of God. This passage highlights the spiritual consequences that can result from engaging in sexual sin.

3. **Destruction and Death**: Proverbs 7:23, 26 (ASV) describes the dire consequences of falling into the trap of sexual

immorality. It portrays the destructive nature of such behavior, leading to ruin and even death. This serves as a warning against the devastating effects that immorality can have on one's life.

4. **Deceptive Nature of Immorality**: Proverbs 9:13-18 (ESV) contrasts the invitations of Wisdom and Folly. The invitation of Folly, which represents sexual immorality, may seem enticing and pleasurable but ultimately leads to destruction and death. This passage highlights the deceptive nature of sexual sin and its detrimental impact on one's life.

These Scriptures emphasize the importance of avoiding sexually immoral conduct. They highlight the value of marital fidelity, the spiritual consequences of sexual sin, the destructive nature of immorality, and the deceptive allure that can lead individuals astray. By adhering to God's standards and embracing purity, believers can experience the blessings of a healthy, committed, and God-honoring sexual life within the confines of marriage.

Why is viewing pornography extremely harmful? (Col. 3:5; Jas. 1:14-15)

Harmfulness of Viewing Pornography

1. **Idolatry and Immorality**: Colossians 3:5 (ASV) warns against the indulgence of sexual immorality and impure desires, categorizing it as idolatry. Viewing pornography involves seeking sexual gratification outside the boundaries of God's design, leading to the worship of one's own desires and the degradation of God's intended purpose for human sexuality.

2. **The Cycle of Temptation and Sin**: James 1:14-15 (ESV) describes the progression from desire to sin and the devastating consequences that follow. It emphasizes that when one is enticed by their own desires and gives in to them, it gives birth to sin. This progression ultimately leads to spiritual death. Viewing pornography can fuel and intensify sinful desires, contributing to a cycle of temptation and sin.

Viewing pornography is extremely harmful for several reasons. It involves engaging in sexual immorality, which is categorized as idolatry and goes against God's design for human sexuality. Additionally, it perpetuates a cycle of temptation and sin, leading to spiritual death. It is essential for believers to recognize the harmful nature of pornography and actively strive to reject and resist its allure, seeking purity and holiness in their thoughts and actions. By relying on the power of the Holy Spirit and filling their minds with God's truth, individuals can overcome the harmful influence of pornography and cultivate a life that honors God.

How do we show that we are on guard against sexually arousing images? (Matt. 5:28-29)

Being On Guard Against Sexually Arousing Images

In Matthew 5:28-29 (ESV), Jesus addresses the issue of lust and emphasizes the importance of guarding our hearts and minds against sexually arousing images:

"But I say to you that everyone who looks at a woman with lustful intent has already committed adultery with her in his heart. If your right eye causes you to sin, tear it out and throw it away. For it is better that you lose one of your members than that your whole body be thrown into hell."

1. **Guarding our Thoughts and Desires**: Jesus teaches that merely looking at someone with lustful intent is equivalent to committing adultery in the heart. This highlights the significance of being vigilant and proactive in guarding our thoughts and desires. We must be aware of the potential for sexually arousing images to lead us astray and take steps to prevent them from entering our minds.

2. **Taking Drastic Measures**: Jesus uses strong language to emphasize the seriousness of the issue. He suggests that if our eyes or any other body part cause us to sin, we should be willing to take drastic measures to eliminate that source of temptation.

This radical statement underscores the importance of prioritizing purity and holiness above all else.

To show that we are on guard against sexually arousing images, we must cultivate a mindset that values purity and actively takes steps to prevent exposure to such content. This involves being mindful of the media we consume, setting boundaries for ourselves, and being willing to make sacrifices to protect our hearts and minds. By filling our minds with God's Word, seeking accountability, and relying on the power of the Holy Spirit, we can effectively guard against sexually arousing images and pursue a life of holiness.

Why do we need to recognize that God strongly disapproves of pornography? (Ex. 19:5)

Recognizing God's Strong Disapproval of Pornography

In Exodus 19:5 (ASV), God establishes His covenant with the Israelites and expresses His expectations for them:

"Now therefore, if ye will obey my voice indeed, and keep my covenant, then ye shall be mine own possession from among all peoples; for all the earth is mine."

1. **God's Ownership and Authority**: God declares that the earth and everything in it belong to Him. As the Creator and Sovereign Lord, He has the ultimate authority over all things, including human behavior and moral standards.

2. **Obedience and Covenant**: God establishes a covenant with His people, emphasizing the importance of obedience to His voice and the keeping of His covenant. This indicates that God desires His people to live in accordance with His commands and principles, including the rejection of behaviors that contradict His will.

From this understanding, we can recognize that God strongly disapproves of pornography because it goes against His principles and moral standards. Pornography promotes sexual immorality, objectification, and lustful desires, which are contrary to God's design for human sexuality within the context of marriage and mutual love and respect.

As followers of God, we are called to honor and respect our bodies, viewing them as temples of the Holy Spirit (1 Corinthians 6:19-20). Engaging in or supporting pornography not only disrespects ourselves but also dishonors God and undermines the sanctity of human relationships. By recognizing God's disapproval of pornography, we are motivated to seek purity, guard our hearts and minds, and pursue righteousness in all areas of our lives.

What are those who produce or promote pornography doing? (Rom. 1:24-27)

Actions of Those Who Produce or Promote Pornography

In Romans 1:24-27 (ESV), the apostle Paul describes the downward spiral of humanity's moral degradation:

"Therefore God gave them up in the lusts of their hearts to impurity, to the dishonoring of their bodies among themselves, because they exchanged the truth about God for a lie and worshiped and served the creature rather than the Creator, who is blessed forever! Amen. For this reason, God gave them up to dishonorable passions. For their women exchanged natural relations for those that are contrary to nature; and the men likewise gave up natural relations with women and were consumed with passion for one another, men committing shameless acts with men and receiving in themselves the due penalty for their error."

1. **Exchanging Truth for a Lie**: Those who produce or promote pornography participate in the exchange of truth for a lie. They distort and pervert the truth about God's design for human sexuality and replace it with a counterfeit narrative that promotes lust, objectification, and sexual immorality.

2. **Dishonoring the Body**: Pornography dishonors the bodies of individuals involved by reducing them to objects of sexual desire and exploiting them for personal gratification. It

disregards the inherent dignity and worth of each person, treating them as mere commodities.

3. **Contrary to Natural Relations**: Paul highlights the perversion of natural relations between men and women that occurs in pornography. It promotes and glorifies sexual activities that are contrary to God's intended design and order.

4. **Consumed by Dishonorable Passions**: Those involved in producing or promoting pornography become consumed by dishonorable passions. Their actions reflect a deepening immersion into immoral behaviors, perpetuating a cycle of sexual degradation and indulgence.

The passage emphasizes the serious consequences of exchanging God's truth for a lie and engaging in sexually immoral practices. Those who produce or promote pornography contribute to the erosion of moral values, the objectification of individuals, and the distortion of God's intended design for human sexuality. As believers, we are called to reject such actions, promote purity, and uphold the sanctity of human relationships as designed by God.

What if you have successfully stopped viewing pornography, but the memories of it return from time to time? (1 Cor. 9:27; Psalm 119:37; Isaiah 52:11; Matthew 5:28; Ephesians 5:3; Colossians 3:5; 1 Thessalonians 4:4-8)

Dealing with the Return of Memories from Past Pornography

It is not uncommon for individuals who have successfully stopped viewing pornography to experience the return of memories from their past struggles. These memories can be distressing and challenging to deal with. Here are some insights from Scripture that can provide guidance and support:

1. **Maintain Self-Discipline**: In 1 Corinthians 9:27 (ESV), the apostle Paul speaks of the importance of self-discipline in the Christian life: "But I discipline my body and keep it under control, lest after preaching to others I myself should be disqualified." Self-discipline involves actively managing one's thoughts, desires, and behaviors. When memories of pornography arise, exercise self-discipline by redirecting your focus, engaging in positive activities, and seeking God's strength to resist temptation.

2. **Pray for God's Help**: Psalm 119:37 (ASV) expresses a prayer for purity: "Turn away mine eyes from beholding vanity, and quicken me in thy ways." When memories of pornography resurface, turn to God in prayer, asking Him to guard your eyes and mind from being captivated by empty and impure thoughts. Seek His strength to walk in His ways and pursue holiness.

3. **Flee Temptation**: Isaiah 52:11 (ESV) urges believers to separate themselves from anything that defiles: "Depart, depart, go out from there; touch no unclean thing; go out from the midst of her; purify yourselves." When memories of pornography resurface, intentionally distance yourself from any triggers or situations that may lead you back into temptation. Flee from circumstances or environments that can compromise your purity and well-being.

4. **Guard Your Thoughts**: Matthew 5:28 (ESV) teaches about the importance of guarding one's thoughts and desires: "But I say to you that everyone who looks at a woman with lustful intent has already committed adultery with her in his heart." When memories of pornography return, be vigilant in guarding your thought life. Reject lustful thoughts, renew your mind with God's truth, and focus on things that are pure, honorable, and praiseworthy (Philippians 4:8).

5. **Walk in Purity**: Ephesians 5:3 (ESV) calls believers to a life of purity: "But sexual immorality and all impurity or covetousness must not even be named among you, as is proper among

saints." As memories of pornography resurface, reaffirm your commitment to live a life of sexual purity. Seek to honor God with your body and maintain integrity in your thoughts and actions.

6. **Put Off Old Desires**: Colossians 3:5 (ESV) instructs believers to put to death their earthly desires: "Put to death therefore what is earthly in you: sexual immorality, impurity, passion, evil desire, and covetousness, which is idolatry." When memories of pornography resurface, remind yourself that those desires are part of your old self that you have put to death in Christ. Choose to live in the freedom and purity found in Him.

7. **Live in Holiness**: 1 Thessalonians 4:4-8 (ESV) encourages believers to live in holiness and control their bodies: "that each one of you know how to control his own body in holiness and honor, not in the passion of lust like the Gentiles who do not know God." When memories of pornography return, remember your calling to live in holiness. Seek to control your body and honor God with your actions.

In dealing with the return of memories from past pornography, it is crucial to rely on God's strength, maintain self-discipline, guard your thoughts, and actively pursue a life of purity and holiness. Seek support from fellow believers, accountability partners, and appropriate resources that can provide guidance and encouragement along your journey towards freedom and healing.

What if on some occasion the desire to view or think about immoral things becomes almost unbearable? (1 Pet. 2:21; Matt. 4:1-11; Phil. 4:6-7)

Dealing with Unbearable Desires for Immoral Things

At times, the desire to view or think about immoral things may become almost unbearable. In these moments of intense temptation, it is crucial to turn to God for strength, guidance, and deliverance. Here are some insights from Scripture that can provide encouragement and support:

1. **Follow the Example of Christ**: 1 Peter 2:21 (ESV) encourages believers to follow the example of Christ in resisting temptation: "For to this you have been called, because Christ also suffered for you, leaving you an example, so that you might follow in his steps." When facing overwhelming desires, remember that Jesus Himself experienced intense temptation during His time on earth. He overcame temptation by relying on the Word of God and remaining obedient to the Father. Follow His example by seeking strength and guidance from God's Word.

2. **Draw Strength from Scripture**: Matthew 4:1-11 (ESV) recounts the temptation of Jesus in the wilderness. When Satan tempted Him, Jesus responded with Scripture, saying, "It is written..." In moments of unbearable desires, immerse yourself in the Word of God. Meditate on passages that speak of purity, righteousness, and the power of God to overcome temptation. Allow God's Word to renew your mind and provide the strength to resist.

3. **Pray and Seek God's Help**: Philippians 4:6-7 (ESV) teaches believers to bring their anxieties and desires before God in prayer: "do not be anxious about anything, but in everything by prayer and supplication with thanksgiving let your requests be made known to God. And the peace of God, which surpasses all understanding, will guard your hearts and your minds in Christ Jesus." When facing overwhelming desires, pour out your heart to God in prayer. Share your struggles, fears, and temptations with Him. Seek His help, surrendering your desires to His control. As you pray, trust that God's peace will guard your heart and mind.

In times of unbearable desires for immoral things, remember that God is faithful and provides a way of escape from every temptation (1 Corinthians 10:13). Seek the support of fellow believers, engage in activities that redirect your focus, and rely on the power of the Holy

Spirit within you to overcome. God's grace is sufficient, and He will enable you to resist temptation and walk in obedience to Him.

Addressing pornography addiction involves understanding the reasons behind the addiction, the triggers that lead to it, and the person's commitment to overcoming it. Here are some specific questions to guide the conversation:

1. **Do you recognize that you have an issue with pornography?** Acknowledging the problem is the first step in overcoming addiction.

2. **Can you identify what triggers your use of pornography?** This helps to understand the circumstances or feelings that lead to the behavior.

3. **How often do you view pornography?** This can provide an understanding of the severity of the addiction.

4. **Have you tried to stop or control your use of pornography?** Their previous attempts can inform what strategies might be effective or ineffective.

5. **How does your use of pornography affect your daily life, relationships, and mental health?** Understanding the negative impacts can motivate the desire for change.

6. **What emotions or situations make you more likely to turn to pornography?** Identifying emotional triggers can help in developing coping strategies.

7. **Are you ready to make changes to overcome your pornography addiction?** Their readiness and commitment to change are key factors in recovery.

8. **How do you typically cope with stress or negative emotions?** This can reveal whether they lack healthy coping mechanisms.

9. **What support systems do you have in place?** Support from friends, family, or support groups can be crucial in overcoming addiction.

10. **Would you consider seeking professional help, such as a therapist or a counselor, to overcome this addiction?** If the addiction is severe, they might benefit from professional treatment.

These questions should be approached with sensitivity and respect, as discussing such personal issues can be difficult. Remember, overcoming addiction is a process that requires time, commitment, and often professional support.

Overcoming Pornography Addiction Through Biblical Principles and Counsel

Pornography addiction can trap individuals in a cycle of guilt and shame. The path to freedom lies in applying the wisdom and principles found in God's Word and seeking support and counsel from the Christian community.

Biblical Principles for Overcoming Temptation

1 Corinthians 10:13 (ESV) tells us, "No temptation has overtaken you that is not common to man. God is faithful, and he will not let you be tempted beyond your ability, but with the temptation he will also provide the way of escape, that you may be able to endure it." The term "peirasmos," translated as temptation in Greek, signifies both an inward and outward trial. The Scripture assures us that no trial is insurmountable with God's guidance and strength.

The Call to Holiness and Purity

In Ephesians 5:3 (ESV), we read, "But sexual immorality and all impurity or covetousness must not even be named among you, as is proper among saints." The Greek term "akatharsia," translated as impurity, signifies a moral uncleanness—in this case, sexual immorality. In contrast, "hagios," translated as saints, refers to those who are set apart for God's purposes. This scripture underscores the importance of maintaining purity in our thoughts and actions.

Renewing the Mind through God's Word

Romans 12:2 (ESV) instructs us, "Do not be conformed to this world, but be transformed by the renewal of your mind, that by testing you may discern what is the will of God, what is good and acceptable and perfect." The Greek term "anakainōsis," meaning renewal, signifies a complete change for the better. This verse emphasizes the need for continual renewal of the mind through God's Word to resist conforming to worldly desires.

Godly Sorrow Leading to Repentance

2 Corinthians 7:10 (ESV) states, "For godly grief produces a repentance that leads to salvation without regret, whereas worldly grief produces death." The Greek term "metanoia," translated as repentance, implies a change of mind and direction. It is essential to approach our shortcomings with a godly sorrow that leads to a genuine change of heart.

Cognitive Behavioral Therapy (CBT) Approach to Overcoming Pornography Addiction

Understanding Triggers and Avoidance Strategies

CBT teaches the identification of triggers that lead to the addictive behavior. Once these triggers are known, the individual can develop strategies to avoid or cope with them effectively.

Cognitive Restructuring

This CBT technique challenges and changes maladaptive thoughts and beliefs related to pornography addiction. It involves recognizing, challenging, and altering cognitive distortions and unhealthy thought patterns that lead to the addiction.

Developing Healthy Coping Mechanisms

CBT encourages the development of healthy coping mechanisms to replace the addictive behavior. These may include physical activities, hobbies, meditation, or other positive outlets.

Exposure and Response Prevention (ERP)

A specific form of CBT, ERP is designed to help individuals resist the urge to engage in compulsive behavior (in this case, viewing pornography) when confronted with triggers.

Professional Support and Therapy

Engaging in therapy with a professional who is knowledgeable about both CBT and the Christian faith can provide additional support for overcoming addiction.

In conclusion, both the Bible and CBT provide potent resources for overcoming pornography addiction. A combined approach, involving a commitment to Biblical principles and the application of CBT techniques, can lead to lasting change and freedom from addiction. As you journey towards freedom, remember Romans 8:37 (ESV), "In all these things we are more than conquerors through him who loved us." With God's help and our efforts, we can conquer any challenge that comes our way.

CHAPTER 23 How Do You Get Control Over Your Masturbation Habit?

Questions and Answers

How does God feel about secret faults such as masturbation on which we may be working?

God's Perspective on Secret Faults and Working Towards Change

When it comes to secret faults, such as struggles with behaviors like masturbation, it is important to understand how God views these issues and our efforts to overcome them. Here are some insights from Scripture:

1. **God's Desire for Holiness**: Throughout the Bible, God calls His people to live holy lives and to be set apart from the ways of the world (Leviticus 11:44, 1 Peter 1:15-16). God desires that we honor Him with our bodies and keep ourselves pure (1 Corinthians 6:18-20). Therefore, it is essential to acknowledge that God wants us to align our actions with His standards of holiness.

2. **God's Love and Mercy**: God is a loving and merciful God. He knows our weaknesses and is aware of our struggles. Psalm 103:14 (ASV) says, "For he knoweth our frame; He remembereth that we are dust." God understands our human nature and the challenges we face. He is patient and compassionate towards us as we seek to grow and overcome our faults.

3. **The Call to Repentance and Transformation**: God calls us to repentance and invites us to experience transformation

through His grace. Acts 3:19 (ESV) says, "Repent therefore, and turn back, that your sins may be blotted out." This means that when we recognize our faults and sinful behaviors, we can turn to God, seeking His forgiveness and the power to change. God is ready to forgive us and empower us to live according to His will.

4. **Working towards Change**: God desires that we continually strive to overcome our faults and grow in holiness. Philippians 2:12-13 (ESV) says, "Work out your own salvation with fear and trembling, for it is God who works in you, both to will and to work for his good pleasure." As we acknowledge our faults, we can take active steps to address them. This involves relying on God's strength, seeking accountability, renewing our minds with His Word, and actively resisting temptation.

While secret faults like struggles with masturbation may bring feelings of guilt or shame, it is essential to remember that God's love and grace extend to all who seek Him. He desires that we bring our struggles before Him, seeking His help and guidance. As we rely on His strength and actively work towards change, we can experience His transformative power in our lives.

What Scriptural counsel indicates that masturbation is to be avoided?

The Bible and Masturbation: Understanding Scriptural Counsel

The Bible does not explicitly mention the act of masturbation. However, there are principles and teachings within Scripture that provide guidance on sexual purity, self-control, and honoring God with our bodies. Here are some scriptural principles that can be applied to the question of masturbation:

1. **Honoring God with our Bodies**: The Bible emphasizes the importance of honoring God with our bodies. 1 Corinthians 6:19-20 (ESV) states, "Or do you not know that your body is a temple of the Holy Spirit within you, whom you have from

God? You are not your own, for you were bought with a price. So glorify God in your body." This passage teaches us that our bodies are sacred, and we should use them in ways that bring glory to God.

2. **Avoiding Sexual Immorality**: Scripture consistently teaches against sexual immorality, which includes any sexual activity outside the context of marriage. 1 Corinthians 6:18 (ESV) says, "Flee from sexual immorality. Every other sin a person commits is outside the body, but the sexually immoral person sins against his own body." Masturbation can potentially fall within the realm of sexual immorality if it involves lustful thoughts or leads to an unhealthy preoccupation with sexual desires.

3. **Guarding Our Hearts and Minds**: Jesus taught the importance of guarding our hearts and minds against lustful thoughts. Matthew 5:28 (ESV) says, "But I say to you that everyone who looks at a woman with lustful intent has already committed adultery with her in his heart." This principle extends to any form of sexual impurity, including thoughts or actions associated with masturbation.

4. **Self-Control and Renewing the Mind**: Scripture encourages believers to exercise self-control and renew their minds. Romans 12:2 (ASV) urges us, "And be not fashioned according to this world: but be ye transformed by the renewing of your mind." This involves aligning our thoughts and actions with God's standards and seeking His help to resist temptations, including sexual temptations.

While the Bible does not explicitly address masturbation, these scriptural principles guide us in making choices that honor God, promote sexual purity, and cultivate self-control. It is important to approach this topic with prayer, seeking the guidance of the Holy Spirit, and seeking wise counsel from trusted spiritual mentors or counselors within the context of your faith community.

How can a Christian overcome the habit of masturbation? (1 Corinthians 9:26; 1 Peter 1:13; Matthew 5:28; Philippians 4:8; Psalm 97:10; Psalm 119:37; Proverbs 24:10; 1 Corinthians 15:58; 2 Corinthians 4:7; Psalm 62:8; Hebrews 4:16; Proverbs 24:5-6)

Overcoming the Habit of Masturbation: Biblical Guidance

The struggle to overcome the habit of masturbation is a common challenge faced by many Christians. Here are some scriptural principles and practical guidance to help individuals in their journey of overcoming this habit:

1. **Self-Discipline and Control**: 1 Corinthians 9:26 (ESV) encourages believers to exercise self-discipline in all areas of life: "So I do not run aimlessly; I do not box as one beating the air." This verse reminds us of the importance of intentional effort and discipline in overcoming any habit, including masturbation.

2. **Guarding the Mind**: 1 Peter 1:13 (ESV) exhorts believers to "prepare their minds for action": "Therefore, preparing your minds for action, and being sober-minded, set your hope fully on the grace that will be brought to you at the revelation of Jesus Christ." By actively guarding our minds against impure thoughts and intentionally focusing on Christ, we can resist temptations and redirect our thoughts towards godliness.

3. **Addressing Lustful Thoughts**: Matthew 5:28 (ESV) teaches the importance of addressing lustful thoughts: "But I say to you that everyone who looks at a woman with lustful intent has already committed adultery with her in his heart." Recognizing and addressing lustful thoughts and desires is crucial in overcoming the habit of masturbation.

4. **Mental Focus on Godly Things**: Philippians 4:8 (ESV) provides guidance on the type of thoughts to dwell on:

"Finally, brothers, whatever is true, whatever is honorable, whatever is just, whatever is pure, whatever is lovely, whatever is commendable, if there is any excellence, if there is anything worthy of praise, think about these things." By intentionally redirecting our thoughts towards things that are pure, honorable, and praiseworthy, we can cultivate a mindset that opposes impure desires.

5. **Seeking God's Strength**: Overcoming any habit requires relying on God's strength and grace. Psalm 97:10 (ASV) reminds us, "Ye that love Jehovah, hate evil: He preserveth the souls of his saints; He delivereth them out of the hand of the wicked." By seeking God's help and relying on His power, we can find the strength to resist temptations and break free from destructive habits.

6. **Prayer and Seeking God's Help**: Psalm 62:8 (ESV) encourages believers to trust in God at all times and pour out their hearts to Him: "Trust in him at all times, O people; pour out your heart before him; God is a refuge for us." Through prayer and seeking God's guidance, individuals can find comfort, strength, and guidance in their journey of overcoming the habit of masturbation.

7. **Accessing God's Grace**: Hebrews 4:16 (ESV) reminds us of our access to God's grace and mercy: "Let us then with confidence draw near to the throne of grace, that we may receive mercy and find grace to help in time of need." Knowing that we have a loving and forgiving God who offers grace and mercy can provide hope and encouragement as we seek to overcome sinful habits.

8. **Perseverance and Endurance**: 1 Corinthians 15:58 (ESV) encourages believers to stand firm and remain steadfast: "Therefore, my beloved brothers, be steadfast, immovable, always abounding in the work of the Lord, knowing that in the Lord your labor is not in vain." Overcoming the habit of masturbation may require perseverance, endurance, and the support of a community of believers.

9. **Wise Counsel and Support**: Seeking wise counsel and support from mature believers or trusted spiritual mentors can be beneficial in overcoming any habit, including masturbation. Proverbs 24:6 (ESV) says, "For by wise guidance you can wage your war, and in abundance of counselors there is victory." Utilizing the wisdom and support of others can provide valuable insights, accountability, and encouragement.

Remember, overcoming any habit takes time, effort, and reliance on God's strength and grace. Each individual's journey may be unique, and it's important to approach this topic with compassion, seeking the guidance of the Holy Spirit and relying on the principles of Scripture to guide personal decisions and actions.

When trying to help someone overcome a habit of masturbation, it's important to approach the subject with sensitivity, respect, and understanding. Here are some specific questions to guide your conversation:

1. **Do you recognize that your masturbation habit is causing concern or distress?** Acknowledging the issue is often the first step towards managing it.

2. **What usually triggers the desire to masturbate?** Understanding their triggers can help identify patterns and potential strategies for managing the behavior.

3. **How often do you masturbate, and how does it affect your daily life?** This provides a gauge of how much the habit is interfering with normal activities and responsibilities.

4. **Have you noticed any physical, emotional, or relational repercussions from this habit?** Exploring the negative effects can heighten awareness of the need for change.

5. **Have you tried to control or stop your masturbation habit before?** Their past attempts can provide insights into what strategies have or haven't worked for them.

6. **Are you using masturbation as a coping mechanism for stress, loneliness, or other uncomfortable feelings?** If so, they might benefit from learning healthier coping strategies.
7. **Are you ready to make changes to manage this habit?** Their readiness and willingness to change are critical for progress.
8. **What other activities or hobbies could you engage in when you feel the urge to masturbate?** Identifying alternative behaviors can help them manage the habit.
9. **Do you have a support system that you could turn to for help and encouragement?** Support from friends, family, or support groups can be beneficial in managing habits.
10. **Would you consider seeking help from a therapist or counselor to overcome this habit?** If the habit is causing significant distress or interfering with daily life, they might benefit from professional guidance.

Remember, these questions should be asked in a supportive and non-judgmental way. Changing habitual behaviors can take time and often requires professional support.

Overcoming a Habit of Masturbation Through Biblical Principles and Counsel

Habits such as masturbation can sometimes lead to guilt, shame, or a sense of being spiritually adrift. To reestablish spiritual balance, believers must anchor themselves in God's Word and follow the principles it lays out.

God's Expectations of Sexual Purity

In 1 Thessalonians 4:3-5 (ESV), Paul writes, "For this is the will of God, your sanctification: that you abstain from sexual immorality; that each one of you know how to control his own body in holiness and honor, not in the passion of lust like the Gentiles who do not know

God." The term translated as "control" comes from the Greek "skeuos," which can also mean "vessel" or "instrument." In this context, it represents our physical bodies, which we are called to handle with care, maintaining purity and honor.

Renewing Your Mind with God's Word

As previously mentioned, Romans 12:2 (ESV) calls us to renovate our minds. The term for renewal, "anakainōsis," signifies a complete transformation, a metamorphosis that shapes our thoughts and actions to align with God's expectations. Regular immersion in and contemplation of God's Word is key to initiating and sustaining this renewal.

Avoiding Temptation

In Matthew 26:41 (ESV), Jesus advises his disciples to "Watch and pray that you may not enter into temptation. The spirit indeed is willing, but the flesh is weak." The Greek term "peirasmos," for temptation, signifies trials of both a moral and external nature. Avoiding situations that might lead to temptation is one way of honoring Jesus' counsel here.

Fleeing Sexual Immorality

Paul's words in 1 Corinthians 6:18-20 (ESV) are clear: "Flee from sexual immorality. Every other sin a person commits is outside the body, but the sexually immoral person sins against his own body." The word "flee" comes from the Greek verb "pheugo," which implies running away from danger. By consciously avoiding sexual immorality, we honor God with our bodies.

Cognitive Behavioral Therapy (CBT) Approach to Overcoming a Masturbation Habit

Understanding Triggers

Identifying and understanding the triggers that lead to the habit of masturbation is a crucial first step. Once these triggers are recognized, one can work to avoid them or to change one's response.

Cognitive Restructuring

Cognitive restructuring involves identifying and challenging maladaptive thoughts and beliefs that contribute to the habit of masturbation. This might involve recognizing and reshaping negative self-talk or unrealistic expectations.

Behavioral Strategies

CBT also offers behavioral strategies to help manage this habit. This may involve finding healthy and constructive ways to manage stress or seeking out activities that distract from the urge to masturbate.

Mindfulness and Relaxation Techniques

Mindfulness helps foster a greater awareness of one's thoughts and behaviors, while relaxation techniques can aid in reducing the physical arousal that might contribute to the habit. This might include practices like deep breathing, progressive muscle relaxation, or mindfulness meditation.

Professional Help

As with any persistent issue, seeking professional help can be beneficial. This could involve seeking out a therapist who is knowledgeable about both CBT and Christian counseling.

In conclusion, the combination of Biblical counsel and Cognitive Behavioral Therapy provides a powerful framework to overcome the habit of masturbation. Remember the words in Philippians 4:13 (ESV), "I can do all things through him who strengthens me." God's strength is made perfect in our weakness, and with His help and your efforts, victory is possible.

www.ingramcontent.com/pod-product-compliance
Lightning Source LLC
LaVergne TN
LVHW020927090426
835512LV00020B/3248